A Treatise in Phenomenological Sociology

A Treatise in Phenomenological Sociology

Object, Method, Findings, and Applications

Carlos Belvedere

LEXINGTON BOOKS
Lanham • Boulder • New York • London

Published by Lexington Books

An imprint of The Rowman & Littlefield Publishing Group, Inc.
4501 Forbes Boulevard, Suite 200, Lanham, Maryland 20706
www.rowman.com

86-90 Paul Street, London EC2A 4NE

British Library Cataloguing in Publication Information Available

Library of Congress Cataloging-in-Publication Data

Names: Belvedere, Carlos, author.
Title: A treatise in phenomenological sociology : object, method, findings, and
    applications / Carlos Belvedere.
Description: Lanham : Lexington Books, [2021] | Includes bibliographical references.
Identifiers: LCCN 2021042656 (print) | LCCN 2021042657 (ebook) |
    ISBN 9781666906103 (cloth) | ISBN 9781666906127 (paper) | ISBN 9781666906110
(ebook)
Subjects: LCSH: Phenomenological sociology.
Classification: LCC HM494 .B45 2021 (print) | LCC HM494 (ebook) |
    DDC 142/.7--dc23
LC record available at https://lccn.loc.gov/2021042656
LC ebook record available at https://lccn.loc.gov/2021042657

Contents

Acknowledgments

We do not live on our own. We do not think on our own either. Much of what the reader will find in this book would not have come to my mind without the enriching exchange with my mentors, colleagues, and students along the years. Phenomenology is a collective endeavor, and I have learned to practice it in the midst of a community. Institutions are important too, as an expression of those communities.

The institutions that influenced me the most are the Society for Phenomenology and the Human Sciences (SPHS) and the International Alfred Schutz Circle for Phenomenology and Interpretive Social Science (also known as the Schutz Circle, for short). I had first learned from Schutz in my *alma mater*, the Universidad de Buenos Aires, where I wrote my PhD dissertation on "the problem of social phenomenology" in his work. My adviser was Dr. Emilio De Ipola; and the most influential scholars for me at the time were Professors Carlos Prego, Graciela Ralón, and Mario Lipsitz. When first attending the annual meeting of SPHS, I had the feeling that my bibliography came to life. It was a unique experience to finally meet many of the authors I had read while writing my dissertation.

At SPHS I reencountered Lester Embree, to whom Roberto Walton generously had introduced me in Buenos Aires. The annual meetings of the Society gave me the invaluable opportunity to meet him on a regular basis and profit from his always clever and many times humorous interventions. He was an inspiration for me, as for many others. Much of what I wrote in this book is based on his work and motivated by countless small chats in hallways, restaurants, and means of transport. Among many other things, I learned from him that phenomenologists should practice worldly phenomenology in the first person *plural* perspective, because individuals are *abstracta* abstracted form groups, which are *concreta*. Many times, during these years, I needed his advice. I still miss him.

Another gift of life that SPHS offered me was getting to know George Psathas. It was Hisashi Nasu who gently introduced us during the founding meeting of the Schutz Circle, in a lasagna restaurant of his choice. Psathas was truly kind to me, probably because of Hisashi's introducing words and because kindness was a personal quality of his. It would not be excessive to say that this book would not have come to exist without his founding contributions. It was Psathas who first championed the idea that phenomenological sociology must be depicted as a paradigm on its own. He was convincing enough to make a first conference on the topic, edit a wonderful book, start a society (SPHS) and launch a prestigious journal, *Human Studies*, that still is a lighthouse in phenomenological sociology and social phenomenology, currently under the guidance of Martin Endress. Two central claims of this book are taking from Psathas's work: that phenomenological sociology is a paradigm switch in social research, and that Garfinkel's ethnomethodology sprinted from Schutz's ideas and evolved to become an experimentation with the natural attitude. I could not imagine the first time I met him how deeply his ideas would influence me throughout the years.

Hisashi also introduced me to Frances Chaput Waksler. Her ideas are a part of this book, as her gentle manners are a part of my memories. To my knowledge, nobody else noted that constitution processes might well be followed by processes of "unconstitution." This put me to think deeper on important aspects of the method in phenomenological sociology, as her contributions on child-adult interaction made me think deeper on how I was raising my daughter. Is it so hard for we adults to treat kids as interactional partners and social persons? And we share a taste for music, but I will not bother the reader with anecdotes about how to play the guitar and the mandolin, or where to listen to good Cajun music in New Orleans.

Well, it is about time to talk about Hisahi Nasu himself. He was the first phenomenological sociologist I ever met in person. He always kept what I perceived as a kind of proud to be a sociologist. That was inspiring. And he helped me to better understand the distinction between eidetic and historical analysis, which is fundamental for drawing the line between phenomenology as a philosophy and as a social science. I would also like to praise his commitment and his generous contributions to keep alive the Schutzian tradition, to create and promote institutions that support it, and to welcome in new generations.

Not only this book but also my Schutz scholarship would have been much different without Michael Barber's writings and personal advice. *The Elusive Other* was the first of his books that I read. It deeply influenced me, not only in my interpretation of Schutz but also in my research on social discrimination in Buenos Aires. How do we grasp that elusive other? Then, the first time I submitted a paper for SPHS it was him who replied to my emails. I could not believe I was going to meet him in person! The reader will notice that his recent book on the emancipating provinces of religion and humor played an important role in shaping the methodological aspects of this proposal. I hope his writings will keep inspiring people like me for many years to come.

I still remember the first time I saw Kenneth B. Liberman. He made a long exposition on Merleau-Ponty at SPHS, which caused me a deep impression. Then I got the chance to talk to him about Garfinkel—an author that, until then, I thought I knew well . . . Ken was kind enough to spend a few summer weeks in Mar del Plata sharing with me his wisdom, his personal experiences and his unique understanding of what phenomenology and ethnomethodology are meant to be. His book *More Studies in Ethnomethodology* helped me work through some of the most difficult riddles of phenomenological sociology.

SPHS was also a place of encounters. There I met Valerie Malhotra Bentz, whose leadership, leregogic vocation and strong commitment with social change still inspires me. I also met Jerry Williams, a sociologist, a poet, and the best company you can have for an evening beer and chat. He gave me one of the best books in sociology I have ever read, Burke C. Thomason's *Making Sense of Reification*, and helped me to better understand the magnitude of Peter L. Berger's contributions to our discipline. The Society as well as the Circle gave me the chance to keep in touch on a regular basis with my dear colleagues: Jochen Dreher, Andreas Göttlich, and Erik Garret. Also, they sheltered my students: Daniela López, Deborah Motta, and Alexis Gros.

The Schutz Circle had another lucky side effect. It allowed me to keep a long-term conversation with Chung-Chi Yu on phenomenological psychology. Our friendly discussion started in 2005, at the meeting of the Organization of Phenomenological Organizations (OPO) in Lima, Peru. There, Lester introduced him as "our guy in Taiwan." Since then, almost every encounter of the OPO and the Circle found us talking—on the streets of Segovia, New York, and many other cities—about Husserl, Schutz, and phenomenological psychology. Our most recent—but, I hope, not the last—encounter took place in Kaohsiung, Chung-Chi's hometown.

It would not have been possible to keep up all these years of working and continuing dialogue with my colleagues without the funding of Universidad de Buenos Aires, CONICET, Universidad Nacional de General Sarmiento, UBACYT, FONCYT, Fundación Williams, and the continuing support of my dear friend Martín Oliver. And this dialogue would had been frustrated, specially at first, without the dedicated and kindest help from my English teacher and friend, Clare Huish. In a way not strictly metaphorical, she opened the world for me.

The loving care and understanding of my wife Marina and the joy of our little Amalia gave me the strength I needed to accomplish the task. If communities and institutions are essential for us to become who we are and think the way we do, how much more important is it to have a home to return to, a family waiting for you, and the kindest two persons in the world to miss and to love while you are away. . . . Thank you for all these years. And for the years to come.

Introduction

Is There Such a Thing as a Phenomenological Sociology?

For some decades now, there has been much ado about phenomenological sociology. Something odd happens. Its supporters as well as its detractors mostly agree that there is not such a thing as a phenomenological sociology. Some believe that, as a philosophy, phenomenology does not belong to the sciences, as sociology does. Some others believe that sociologists work with different methods and deal with different objects than phenomenologists, so they perform quite different activities. Incredibly, everybody is willing to enthusiastically discuss about something which (so they believe) does not exist.

On the contrary, this book aims at stating categorically that phenomenological sociology exists. However, this statement is not as evident as it might seem since phenomena and their study are never given spontaneously but through the rigors of a disciplined method. It is neither an indisputable statement since, as I said, the idea of a phenomenological sociology has been called into question for some time. Yet, the debate has helped to keep an open horizon for this collective task that, just like phenomenological philosophy, is always starting anew. For this reason, the state of perpetual deliberation does not reveal the impossibility but rather the renewed fertility of phenomenological sociology.

A VAGUE IDEA ABOUT PHENOMENOLOGICAL SOCIOLOGY

The debate about the possibility of a phenomenological sociology has been centered around the Schutzian tradition. Curiously, Schutz never ever used the expression "phenomenological sociology." Notwithstanding, well respected sociologists and phenomenologists have written on Schutz's "phenomenological sociology." However, most references to Schutz's alleged "phenomenological sociology" are vague and uncertain.

See, for instance, how Hindess manages to write a paper on "The 'phenomenological' sociology of Alfred Schutz"—where he states that "Schutz's work is frequently said to have laid the foundations of a phenomenological sociology (2006, 6)—without saying a word about what we should understand by it. He only discusses Schutz's phenomenology and Schutz's methodology of the social sciences, not his alleged phenomenological sociology. In other words, under the heading of "phenomenological sociology," Hindess addresses a number of subjects, none of which strictly belongs to phenomenological sociology.

Overgaard and Zahavi are also vague while writing about phenomenological sociology in Schutz, even if one main difference can be established with Hindess: that they actually include in their paper important issues of phenomenological sociology,[1] the problem being that they are presented along with problems pertaining to other phenomenological disciplines without making an appropriate distinction of the different layers of experience involved. The problem seems to be taking what Schutz said about phenomenology and the social sciences at large as valid for phenomenological sociology in particular.

Indeed, one of the main confusions consists in taking both domains as if they were the same, thus transferring much of what Schutz said about the social sciences to sociology—for example, the epistemological question of the "constructs of the second degree" (Overgaard and Zahavi 2009, 100). Another important misunderstanding consists in assuming that, for Schutz, "sociology" means "phenomenological sociology" while he often refers to other sociologists' perspectives. An example of this kind of improper inferences is to think that sociality is important for phenomenological sociology just because it is "a central theme in phenomenology" (Overgaard and Zahavi 2009, 93). Not that it is not. It matters for all social and human sciences. In other words, it is not specifically sociological.

In addition, Overgaard and Zahavi miss a number of distinctions that Schutz himself made, which are important to understand how he related phenomenology and the sciences. For instance, main issues of phenomenological psychology such as the natural attitude, intersubjectivity and the thesis of the reciprocity of perspectives are considered instead as problems of phenomenological sociology (Overgaard and Zahavi 2009, 93, 103, 105).

Making this clear is important because, according to Schutz, phenomenological psychology is fundamental regarding all human and social sciences—including phenomenological sociology, if I may say. Yet, Overgaard and Zahavi overlook this distinction—in a way not so different to Hindess, after all, since in both perspectives the social sciences seem to deal with an extensive, undifferentiated range of problems.

Actually, Overgaard and Zahavi include in their presentation of phenomenological sociology a wide scope of subjects which in fact are common to all human and social sciences, making no distinctions of order, grounding, or priority among them. Assorted matters are mentioned one after the other, without making explicit their orderliness; for instance: social reality as "a product of human activity" (Overgaard and Zahavi 2009, 93), sociality as intersubjectivity (Overgaard and Zahavi 2009, 96, 101), the different provinces of meaning (Overgaard and Zahavi 2009, 99), and the congruence of the systems of relevances (Overgaard and Zahavi 2009, 103).

Even though all these issues are important to sociology, not all of them are strictly sociological. They belong to the larger domain of social phenomenology.[2] Of course they are related to sociology, but they are not a part of it. Let us take, for instance, the life-world: it is right to say that the sociologist "should take her point of departure" in it and provide for "a systematic examination of everyday life." But it is only the point of departure, not the content of sociological theory, neither the result of sociological inquiries. In a more phenomenological language, we should say that sociology is grounded in the life-world; but phenomenology has much more to offer than just setting a starting point. It has specific contributions to sociology, not just general reflections helpful to a number of disciplines. It is unfair to claim that Schutz's legacy to sociology is "to describe and analyze the essential structures of the life-world" and to account for "the way in which subjectivity is involved in the construction of the social meaning, social actions and situations—indeed social 'worlds'" (Overgaard and Zahavi 2009, 100). Certainly those are major contributions, but the life-world is supposed to be the ground for all sciences and even for philosophy; subjectivity plays an important role in all human activities; and any social science is involved with meaning, actions, situations, and social worlds. Therefore, arguing that, "in Schutz's view, sociology should focus on the life-world as it is experienced by everyday subjects" (Overgaard and Zahavi 2009, 107), does not say much about sociology in particular. So, we need a more specific definition of what phenomenological sociology is.

WHAT IS PHENOMENOLOGICAL SOCIOLOGY? A DEBATE

Sociology and phenomenology can be seen either as different disciplines related to one another, or as one integrated albeit complex field of research: "Either phenomenology and sociology are interpreted as two different enterprises that, however, can be related, or a 'synthesis' is proclaimed under the label of a phenomenological sociology. The first approach interprets Schutz's life-world analysis as protosociology, the second one as sociology" (Eberle 2012, 135). One is introduced by Thomas Luckmann, the second one is started by George Psathas.[3] Luckmann's stance considers that phenomenology is not a sociology because it is a philosophy and not a science. Accordingly, he assumes that phenomenology can ground sociology, but it cannot be a part of it. Psathas's position, instead, maintains that phenomenology is a way of doing sociology. Accordingly, no matter how important it might be for philosophy, phenomenology has much to say in the realm of sociology—with one important condition: that sociology does not remain the same as before meeting phenomenology. Let us consider each of these claims in some detail.

On one hand, for Luckmann, phenomenology is a philosophy. Consequently, it can only be presociological or protosociological because sociology is an empirical science. As they proceed through two completely different methods, a phenomenological sociology is a misnomer because phenomenology is not a science but a philosophy dealing with phenomena of subjective consciousness from an egological perspective. Alternatively, as a science, sociology deals with phenomena of the social world from a cosmological perspective. Thus, as Eberle puts it, either you do phenomenology or you do sociology, even though they are compatible given that the basic structures of the life-world serve as a protosociology, and sociological concepts refer to those basic structures.

Unlike Eberle, who considers that beyond their differences both positions maintain that phenomenology is productive for sociology, Dreher (2012) is skeptical regarding the idea that phenomenology and sociology are compatible. By making Luckmann's stance his own, he argues that "phenomenological sociology" is an oxymoron because it refers to distinct disciplines with different methodological directions. Phenomenology is an egological discipline whose aim is to describe how the objects and the social world are constituted in consciousness. Consequently, it is a protosociology but not a sociology because the latter is an eidetic mundane science dealing with cultural and social phenomena and based on a theory of science, not on a philosophy.

From this viewpoint, protosociology is seen as a link between the universal subjective structures and the objective historical and social structures. This means, for Dreher, that the social scientist is always confronted with meaning structures already analyzed in detail by previous phenomenological investigations; that is to say, that phenomenological description serves to analyze the epistemological basis of sociology.

This way of understanding the relationship between sociology and phenomenology certainly requires a kind of linkage between the two of them. Dreher invokes here the notion of "parallel action." This expression intends to describe the interplay of phenomenology and the social science, based on the concepts of "constitution" and "construction." Constitution "refers to the constitutive processes of the subjective consciousness that are the basis for building up the individual's world"; construction, instead, "refers to concrete sociohistorical expressions of the world as well as specific phenomena which are socially 'constructed'" (Dreher 2012, 154). Seen this way, there is no phenomenological sociology; at most, we can relate and corroborate, in a parallel action, findings in the social sciences (which deal with the social construction of phenomena) with findings in phenomenology (which deals with their constitution in consciousness).

No matter how distinguished supporters it has had, this viewpoint is quite perplexing. It creates more difficulties than it solves. Indeed, it seeks an alternative to mainstream sociology (which is good) at the expense of making it dependent upon transcendental philosophy—i.e., it aims at establishing it as a distinctive endeavor which, however, ends up being dependent of a different discipline. In addition, how could there be an authentic parallel between empirical and transcendental, contingent and necessary phenomena? And how could historical facts be the exact parallel of irreal essences? Not only is the parallelism blurred but also the idea of phenomenology, which ends up being a kind of neither social nor historical discipline.

From a different angle, phenomenology can be seen as a sociological paradigm alternative to positivistic sociology. This was clearly noted by George Psathas in his exhaustive, sharp, and visionary introduction to *Phenomenological Sociology*. In his view, phenomenology is not only a philosophy but also a method and a perspective in the social sciences. As a part of this perspective, phenomenological sociology is a paradigm which includes not only "applications" but also "programmatic statements" (Psathas 1973, 2).

Indeed, Psathas describes the phenomenological approach in sociology as "a new paradigm that offers an alternative to the restricted potential of positivist perspectives" which can provide "a fresh, open, and innovative approach [. . .] avoiding preconceived sociological notions and concepts as well as the established recipes and formulas of research procedures" (Eberle 2012, 139). In other words, phenomenological sociology is a *new* paradigm and an *alternative* to positivist approaches.

In this line of argument, Waksler observes that phenomenological sociology "works with different assumptions than positivist science," and that "it questions implicit assumptions about reality and knowledge with which sociologists operate" (Eberle 2012, 143). Thus, its goal is not just to provide a philosophical foundation of the social sciences but to reach new sociological insights. Once sociologists reach new insights, they can discover or create new relationships with fresh perspectives.

Phenomenological sociology not only leads to a paradigm switch but also allows the new sciences to relate to philosophy in a different way. This means that it not only changes the way sociology interacts with other disciplines but also the way it relies on philosophical groundings. For instance, one might look to the field of transcendental consciousness which, according to Barber, frequently remains implicit in ethnomethodological analysis. In his perspective, "the transcendental ego simply represents the final standpoint to which one's reflectivity leads, a reflectivity engaged in making explicit what is implicit in everyday life situations, as ethnomethodology has done so well, or in the activity of the ethnomethodologists themselves, who, in abandoning any theory aloof from everyday life, risk submerging their own perspective in the everyday life situation investigated" (Barber 2012, 83).

In this perspective, Psathas's stance can be contrasted with Luckmann's, whose standpoint seems to start from the unexamined assumption that, as phenomenology is external to sociology, it might ground it without major consequences. If, however, phenomenology and sociology cannot be merged, it is not clear how phenomenology could influence sociology in a profound way. Although the grounding of the sciences has always been an important task for phenomenology, it has also looked for their renewal. In this regard, one may be skeptical about the potential of Luckmann's position in this debate to promote a deep renewal of sociology as a science since it does not question old-fashioned positivistic divisions of scientific labor. If phenomenology must limit itself to grounding science, how could it lead to an internal critique of its unexamined assumptions?

Instead, Psathas argues that phenomenology can be a manner of doing sociology which changes the way we practice it by questioning old-fashioned positivistic assumptions. In his perspective, phenomenological sociology is "a new paradigm that offers an alternative to the restricted potential of positivist perspectives" and offers "a fresh, open, and innovative approach [. . .] avoiding preconceived sociological notions and concepts as well as the established recipes and formulas of research procedures" (Eberle 2012, 139).

THE IDEA OF PHENOMENOLOGICAL SOCIOLOGY IN THE SCHUTZIAN TRADITION

Which side shall we take, Luckmann's or Psathas's? To make a choice, I will go back to Schutz's work, the godfather or the tradition amid which we are posing this question. Even though—as I said—he never used the expression "phenomenological sociology," he did mention "philosophical sociology," and—as we know—he thought of philosophy as no different to phenomenology. Does this suffice to say that he was a phenomenological sociologist *strictu sensu*? I mean, can we find in philosophical sociology something else than just a protosociology? My answer is: yes and no; so, not fully.

On one side, the tasks of philosophical sociology—as defined in the rare passages in which Schutz mentions it—are: (a) to account for "the structuring of the social world" (Schutz 1966, 118–119); (b) to study the modifications which the "systems of relevancy pertaining to fellow-men in face-to-face situations undergo in the interpretations of the world of predecessors and anticipations of the world of successors" (Schutz 1966, 132); and (c) "to develop a typology of the forms of getting-together and living-together characteristic of the constitution of the various social units, and to determine their order of rank" (Schutz 1966, 178). So, yes: these subject matters are sociological and have been put by Schutz into phenomenological terms. Then, it would be sound to argue that they can be the object of phenomenological sociology.

On the other side, Schutz himself considered that at least one of these issues—namely, "c"—belongs to philosophical sociology but not to sociology. Thus, not every subject pertaining to one domain belongs to the other. Take, for instance, Max Scheler, one of the major inspirations of philosophical sociology. Schutz argues that, in his latter works—"of mainly sociological content"—Scheler "rejected or at least considerably modified his earlier theories" outlined in his ethics by transforming "his theory of perspectivism of values into a new and highly original approach to a sociology of knowledge" (Schutz 1966, 178). So, no: even if "philosophy" could be interpreted as "phenomenology," the scope and reach of "philosophical sociology" are larger than sociology's, which leads us to conclude that they are not the same.

In short, even if some matters of what could be thought of as "phenomenological sociology" are a part of "philosophical sociology," they are, precisely, only a part of it. Moreover, philosophical sociology is to some extent a philosophical grounding of sociology closer to Luckmann's conception of protosociology than to Psathas's idea of phenomenological sociology as a scientific stance. Therefore, it is not phenomenological sociology as we understand it. Though, it tells us something about it: that it does not suffice to relate phenomenology and sociology to have an authentic phenomenological sociology. What is needed is that phenomenology becomes a part of sociology, not just a fundament or a starting point. That, we can find it—once again—in Schutz's comments on Scheler.

According to Schutz, Scheler had to modify his philosophical theories about society in order to have a "sociological insight into the relativistic structure of the human condition" (Schutz 1966, 134) and make his "remarkable contribution to the foundation of the sociology of knowledge" (Schutz 1966, 142–143). Thus, Scheler's contributions to sociology did not come from his philosophical ideas but from a fresh sociological perspective.

Something similar happened to Schutz himself. His sociology is a fruition of maturity, which is better presented in his latest writings and seminars.

Of particular importance is Schutz's course on the sociology of language (2010), the last that he taught at the Graduate Faculty of the New School for Social Research (Kersten 2010, 61). There, what Scheler called the "relative natural conception of the world" plays a main role in defining the task of a sociology of knowledge; namely,

> to see how different things are taken for granted in various historical periods in various situations [. . .] In addition, the sociologist of knowledge should also consider situations where what is taken for granted is questioned, where the whole relative natural conception of the world is questioned. (Schutz 2010, 92)

Briefly said, the sociology of knowledge deals with "the underlying relative natural conception of the world" of a group of people, with "their common, unquestioned beliefs, attitudes and forms of behavior" (Schutz 2010, 64).

In its turn, "the conception is 'natural' because it is largely taken for granted, as a matter of course, without question" (Schutz 2010, 64). In other words, the relative natural conception of the world has to do with our accepting or taking for granted the world we live in, which "may involve a certain 'world-view,' a comprehensive behavior and understanding" (Schutz 2010, 64). Indeed, the relatively natural worldview prevailing in a social group "is accepted by its members as the only right, good, and efficient way of life. [. . . It] is taken for granted beyond question by the respective social group and thus accepted as socially approved" (Schutz and Luckmann 1989, 288).

Also, the relative natural conception of the world predetermines what features of the world "are worthy of being expressed, and therewith what qualities of these features and what relations among them deserve attention, and what typifications, conceptualizations, abstractions, generalizations, and idealizations are relevant for achieving typical results by typical means" (Schutz and Luckmann 1989, 288).

So far, then, we have seen Schutz's appreciation for Scheler's sociology of knowledge. Does this have anything to do with phenomenological sociology? Yes, if we set aside most of what Schutz said about the sociology of knowledge while portraying other author's theories—mainly, Mannheim and Scheler—and we focus on what Schutz borrowed from them and rephrased in his own terms. In this light, we can find two reasons why Schutz's comments on Scheler should be taken as contributions to phenomenological sociology: (a) because he considered Scheler a phenomenologist—who was sometimes mistaken, but a phenomenologist after all; and (b) because he approached Scheler's natural conception of the world as a "group phenomenon" (Schutz

2010, 63), thus fulfilling both requirements of phenomenological sociology: that of being sociological and that of being phenomenological.

AIMS AND SCOPE OF THIS BOOK

The aim of this book is to outline the program of phenomenological sociology. The claim is that phenomenological sociology exists not only as a matter of fact but also as a meaningful idea. The evidence provided will concern three aspects that, since the uprise of modern science, have been considered canonic criteria to assess the alleged scientific status of a discipline; namely, that it has a specific object, a method of its own, and an established body of concepts—which in this book will be better addressed as "findings." Also, since new scientific domains were often established by detaching themselves from the philosophical approach to their realm of study, the relationship among both fields is a relevant aspect to be considered.

In the following chapters, I will address each of these subjects, starting with the philosophical bases of phenomenological sociology. I will find those bases in the work of Alfred Schutz and, consequently, in the phenomenological perspective started by Edmund Husserl. Schutz interpreted Husserl's legacy in a faithful although creative way. It is unlikely that phenomenological sociology would have come to exist without the amazing work of elaboration attained by Schutz. Not only conceptually but also historically, phenomenological sociology sprints off form his ideas.

Accordingly, chapter 1 will be devoted to present, in a systematic, concise way, some fundamental aspects of Schutz's phenomenology. The focus will be set on the methodological aspects of the *epoché*, the reduction, and the constitutional aspects of the natural attitude as Schutz conceived them, in his own peculiar way. In a wider view, appreciations of how Schutz conceived the global drive of phenomenology will be provided, since phenomenological sociologists found in them much of their inspiration.

Chapter 2 will deal with the specific object of phenomenological sociology. The claim will be that phenomenological sociology is a science of the natural attitude of groups. Its goal is to describe how this attitude is constituted, which involves—among other things—to study what is taken for granted by a given group and how the natural attitude of its members is structured as a worldview. This requires, on the one hand, considering what aspects are they taking for granted, what other aspects they cannot come to think, and which of those aspects they are able to call into question. On the other hand, it involves—as its main task and ultimate accomplishment—the description of the congregational work of making sense of reality, producing a local order which becomes evident for its members. The specific description of the methods, theories, and resources applied to this end is one of the most peculiar and groundbreaking contributions of phenomenological sociology.

In chapter 3, the matter addressed will be the method. In phenomenological sociology, it comprises three fundamental steps; namely, the description of the natural attitude of a given group and its *epoché*, the eidetic description of the constancies constituted in that attitude seen from a worldly perspective, and the disclosure of the work of constitution of those constancies as a group accomplishment. Not only theoretical definitions will be given but also examples taken from classic and contemporary social thinkers who have performed on their own each of these steps.

Chapter 4 will provide a compendium of the fundamental findings in the Schutzian tradition concerning main issues of phenomenological sociology. There is much more to this tradition than what could fit in one chapter. The focus will be on a set of core issues which, in the author's view, conform the backbone of social ontology. Six topics will be addressed. The first and fundamental is the *ego agens* as de *hipokeimenon* (or substratum) of social reality. The second one will be *pragmata* as the ego's workings, one of whose distinctive features is reiterability. Third, habitualities will be considered as consequence of the reiterability and the transferability of *pragmata* that produces a sedimentation of meaning in the social self, which are new acquisitions of the *ego agens*. Fourth, social personalities will be depicted as originated in the split of the temporality of the *ego agens* in *durée* (or inner time) and public time, and in the split of this *ego* in multiple selves that it uses to interact in different social circles. This leads to the fifth subject, social roles. To interact in social life, the ego—endowed with multiple social personalities—must assume different roles, which are typified forms of behavior sanctioned by the group. Sixth, and last, when those patterns are held over time, they can start social institutions, which are standardized patterns of social behavior whose human origin have been forgotten and thus end up being reified and mystified.

Seen as a whole, these chapters will demonstrate that—as argued from the start in this book—phenomenological sociology produces a paradigm switch. I hope they work as a convincing piece of evidence for the reader. The backbone of the argument is that, having an object of its own, a specific method, and a corpus of findings, phenomenological sociology has succeeded in establishing a new, distinct scientific perspective.

WHAT IS PHENOMENOLOGICAL SCIENCE?

Phenomenological sociology belongs to the field of "scientific phenomenologies" as advocated by Giorgi (2020, 135), whose aim is to oppose to the hegemonic empiricism from a new, "non-naturalistic framework" (Giorgi 2020, 157). In this view, when we—phenomenological sociologists—claim our right to be considered scientists, we make a specific claim. We do not mean to be scientific as in mainstream sociology. In phenomenological sociology, our paradigm finds its bases in the philosophy of Alfred Schutz, as will be exposed in chapter 1. By now, all we need to know is that phenomenological science—as most sciences do—works on two different, although related, levels: one rational, another, empirical.

It might seem that this distinction matches the positivist division of the theoretical and the empirical. It does not. First, because phenomenology is not a theoretical stance; second, because it considers experience in an in-depth, thick perspective which goes way beyond what the empiricists would admit. Let us consider each of these motives in some detail.

Many positivists think of phenomenology as nonscientific. At least two different meanings are attached to this perception. Some believe that phenomenology is a philosophy, not a science. Some others, instead, are willing to admit that phenomenology belongs to the sciences but only as a theoretical approach lacking any specific empirical basis—in other words, they admit that phenomenology can provide concepts, even some good ideas, to the sciences, but then they must pass the test of empirical research in order to be admitted as proper scientific knowledge.

The problem with these perspectives is the strong divide between *theoria* and *empeiria*. Phenomenological concepts are not strictly theoretical, neither the facts considered are deprived of abstract meaning. On the contrary, phenomenology's concepts are the product of abstraction processes rooted in lived experiences. Conceptualization starts with things as encountered in the ongoing affairs of everyday life. The phenomenological sociologist must start from an account of actual, real experiences of ordinary people in factually existing social settings. After painstaking processes of abstraction, he must then return to those experiences in search of scientific validation of the concepts abstracted. This means that—as Schutz insightfully noticed—in our field of research, concepts are typologies of plenitude and not pure, abstracted forms. In other words, concepts must always keep some experiential content.

However, the term "experience" can radically change its meaning when used by the positivist and by the phenomenological scientist. Quite often, mainstream sociology takes experience as collection and analysis of data, where "analysis" means mostly quantification. It is not that phenomenological sociologist have a problem with that per se. However, we do have a problem when that means cutting free from the real, worldly experience of what Schutz called "the man on the street." In other words, phenomenological sociology is sensitive to what Husserl (1970, 127ff.) condemned as the "substruction" of the life-world—an endemic bias in "Galilean science," which is a naturalistic, objectivistic approach.

That phenomenological sociology opposes to naturalistic methods does not simply mean that it leans toward interpretive social science. There are many qualitative perspectives in sociology, and phenomenological sociology is one of them, but not *just one of them*. As seen in the first section of this introduction, the mere concern with subjective meaning does not suffice. Subjectivity must be addressed in the first person plural perspective. Also, it must be embedded in the natural attitude, and not that of the individual but of the group. To that aim, not just any qualitative method would do but specifically the methods of the *epoché*, the reduction and constitutional analysis—methods used by no other kind of sociology, qualitative or quantitative.

By the way, in our perspective, the so called "qualitative methods" are not really methods but rather technics for social research. In our view, a method concerns the systematic arrangement of the different moments of the research process viewed as a whole, which must be in accordance with the fundamental claims of a given discipline. In phenomenological sociology, the method is a threefold procedure which—as will be seen in chapter 3—starts by executing the *epoché* of the natural attitude of the group being studied, goes on performing the eidetic variation, and ends up doing constitutional analysis. Different technics such as interviews, participant observation, ethnography, and the like, might serve its purpose. Even quantitative techniques will do, as can be appreciated in Durkheim (2005), where statistics help to establish regularities that contribute to eidetic analysis. Thus, qualitative technics are useful tools for phenomenological sociology as long as they are integrated into its peculiar methodological framework.

The author is aware that, by now, some readers might find it difficult to imagine how this method may work in a concrete situation. I beg them patience. In chapter 3, plenty of examples will be given, including a case study on Tango dancing conducted by the author. The disoriented or the anxious reader might want to skip right to the section "A Case Study (or How This Method Helped Me Through in a Research I Conducted)," in chapter 3.[4] There, one will learn that the *epoché* of the natural attitude of a group can be performed in practical ways, in line with what many sociologists call "to denature" things taken for granted. Once done, unnoticed constancies appear, which are the object of eidetic analysis. Then, one can proceed to describe the congregational work at play in constituting those constancies in that natural attitude which, at first, appeared to us as a given, not yet as an accomplishment.

NOTES

1. The topics of phenomenological sociology listed by Overgaard and Zahavi (2009, 103–104, 106) are mainly related to the sociology of knowledge: its social derivation and distribution, its structural and genetic socialization, and the stocks of typifications, maxims, and recipes of practical know-how.

2. Social phenomenology deals with issues concerning the ontological region of the social in its full extent, starting by the most basic ones such as a non-metaphysical, relational concept of being and the problems of constitution in the natural attitude; then distinguishing different kinds of constituted objectivities, as well as the ontological regions that bring them together and the subjectivity which performs those constitutional acts; finally, focusing on (but not limited to) the distinction of ideal, abstract social objects (such as social relations, social being, and the like) in terms of "society," from the collective constitutional power conceived in terms of "community," both at an eidetic and at an empirical level. Only the latest strata can be strictly called "sociological," while all of them belong to social phenomenology.

3. The reader will find a more detailed study on Psathas's position in this debate in my paper "On George Psathas and Phenomenological Sociology" (Belvedere 2013b).

4. Just like Julio Cortazar's *Rayuela* (2019), this book can be read in different orders, according to the reader's preference.

Chapter One

The Philosophical Bases of Phenomenological Sociology

This book draws its main inspiration from the work of Alfred Schutz. This is not to say that everything it contains is Schutz's explicit sayings; rather, it means that it has a Schutzian spirit.[1] Of course, the following theoretical and philosophical claims are my own; however, I do not intend to say anything "original." Best ideas do not come out of the blue. We always think within established traditions. Pretending no one else ever had a similar idea before is no more than a narcissistic illusion.

Accordingly, the reader will find here no more than what I already found in Schutz and his heirs, even if expressed in my own, idiosyncratic way. At best, one will find a personal way to understand Schutz's legacy, but I cannot even promise that. Irremediably, this is the way I understand phenomenology as a Schutzian true believer.

PHENOMENOLOGY AS "A MERE TECHNICAL DEVICE"

Some of us Schutzians conceive phenomenology as a technical device. Even though Schutz did not explicitly say it, his stance can be interpreted in opposition to Heidegger since he advocates for a technical interpretation of phenomenology,[2] aiming to step away from all mystical ideas toward a rigorous methodological conception according to which phenomenology provides resources to deal with evidence based on mundane procedures in the full sense of the term. In this context, phenomenology does not require any mystical gift but only a scientific and philosophical attitude because, "to the phenomenologist, evidence is not a hidden quality inherent in a specific kind of experience, but the possibility of referring derived experiences to an originary one" (Schutz 1962, 109).

Chapter One

The most important device in phenomenology is the reduction, which Schutz conceived as a mere technique: as "no more than a radicalized renewal of the Cartesian method" consisting in refraining "intentionally and systematically from all judgments related directly or indirectly to the existence of the outer world [. . .] in order to go beyond the natural attitude of man living within the world" (Schutz 1962, 104). This technique consists in an "artificial change from man's attitude in his daily life toward the world and his belief in it to the attitude of the philosopher, who by this very problem is bound to reject any presupposition that does not stand the test of his critical doubt" (Schutz 1962, 104). This switch in attitude makes possible "an investigation within the purified sphere of conscious life, upon which all our beliefs are founded" (Schutz 1962, 104).

Another main phenomenological technique, which Schutz applied in the reduced sphere (egological and not egological) is the eidetic reduction, which allows the phenomenologist to perform "the task of clarification of a complete system of all intuitively knowable essences" (Schutz 1966, 49). So eidetic reduction is "no more than another methodological device of investigation," a mere "methodological device for the solutions of a special task" (Schutz 1962, 113–115). It is only because of the misunderstandings caused by the "unfortunate" metaphysical connotations of terms chosen by Husserl that many readers are induced "to identify the 'essence' with the Platonic idea" or the term *Wesensschau* with some "kind of irrational intuition, like certain techniques of revelation accessible only to the mystic in ecstasy, which is used by the phenomenological esoteric in order to gaze at the eternal truths" (Schutz 1962, 114).

WORLDLY PHENOMENOLOGY

Another hallmark of the Schutzian tradition is defining phenomenology as "worldly" because of his attachment to the natural attitude (see, for instance, Embree 1988). Its goal is to describe the constitution of the natural attitude, without necessarily disconnecting it. Of course, it is possible to put out of work the natural attitude, if you are a philosopher; but that is not required for every exploration of the life-world. In the sciences, one may well describe the constitution of the natural attitude as it is given, without performing the transcendental reduction all the way through. Sure, you will have to practice eidetic analysis, but there is no need to take the transcendental turn and reach for the absolute ego because just stepping back to the monad (or the concrete ego) will suffice. In other words, the scientist can perform eidetic analysis from an egological point of view (see Embree 2009a, 181–183, 204–206, 209; and Belvedere 2013a, 70–71).

Schutz's mundane stance has been objected for being non-phenomenological. Also, his criticism of some results of transcendental phenomenology—particularly of its unsuccessful attempts to account in full for intersubjectivity—have been interpreted as a rejection of transcendental phenomenology. It has been said, for instance, that Schutz's foundation of sociology is not phenomenological because "Husserl's concepts cannot enter the space that Schutz provides for them" (Hindess 2006, 8) and that, in accordance, he "produces a more or less complex psychologistic perversion of transcendental phenomenology which gives an appearance of 'radicality' to Schutz's idealist individualism" (Hindess 2006, 15).

This kind of criticism is baseless. Schutz did not object to transcendental philosophy in principle but only for the sake of convenience, aiming to address some "widespread misunderstandings" such as the idea that it "denies the actual existence of the real life-world, or that it explains it as mere illusion by which natural or positive scientific thought lets itself be deceived" (Schutz 1962, 122).

In this view, the fact that many of Husserl's analyses were carried out in the phenomenologically reduced sphere, and that the problems dealt with become visible only after this reduction is performed, does not impair the validity of their results within the realm of the natural attitude (Schutz 1962, 149). In Schutz's view, "Husserl himself has established once and for all the principle that analyses made in the reduced sphere are valid also for the realm of the natural attitude" (Schutz 1962, 149). Furthermore, he was confident that, since to each empirical determination within the mundane sphere there necessarily corresponds a feature within the aprioristically reduced sphere, "all our discoveries within the reduced sphere will stand the test also in the mundane sphere of our life within the world" (Schutz 1962, 104).

This confidence that "all analyses carried through in phenomenological reduction essentially retain their validation" in the mundane sphere sets the basis of an eidetic mundane science as a "psychological apperception of the natural attitude" which "stands at the beginning of all methodological and theoretical scientific problems of all the cultural and social sciences" (Schutz 1962, 132). Schutz considers that here lies "the tremendous significance of the results achieved by Husserl for all the cultural sciences"[3] and that "the wealth of his analyses pertinent to problems of the *Lebenswelt*" is his "signal contribution to the social sciences" (Schutz 1962, 149).

A DESCRIPTIVE PHENOMENOLOGY
OF THE NATURAL STANCE

Schutz's phenomenology of the natural attitude aims to describe "the world of everyday life that the wide-awake adult, who operates within it and upon it among his fellowmen, experiences as reality" (Schutz and Luckmann 1989, 293). Thus, its starting point is "the analysis of the world of daily life as reality given in the natural attitude of the wide-awake, grown-up man who lives and acts in it and works upon it amid his fellow men" (Schutz 1996, 26). By "wide-awake" Schutz means: "the particular *attention à la vie* of people engaged in carrying out their *pragma* and, accordingly, that attitude of attention and of context of interest to which the highest tension belongs and to it alone" (Schutz 2013, 276).

In this view, the expression "natural attitude" means that "the self simply accepts as real phenomena presented to it without asking whether or not they are truly being or illusion as long as its experiencings of these phenomena are consistent and no event intrudes which would disrupt this consistency" (Schutz 2013, 281). Within the natural attitude we are induced to bestow upon the everyday life-world the accent of reality

> because our practical experiences prove the unity and congruity of the world of working as valid and the hypothesis of its reality as irrefutable. Even more, this reality seems to us to be the natural one, and we are not ready to abandon our attitude toward it without having experienced a specific *shock* which compels us to break through the limits of this "finite" province of meaning and to shift the accent of reality to another one. (Schutz 1962, 231)

Through the natural attitude, then, "I take this world for granted as my reality" (Schutz 1962, 306) and as "the one and unitary world" (Schutz 2013, 281). "I just live along amidst other human beings [. . .] just as I live amidst objects of the outer world" not being aware of myself (Schutz 1962, 168). I am "living in my acts and thoughts, and in doing so, I am exclusively directed towards the objects of my acts and thoughts. Then my stream of thought seems to be an anonymous flux" (Schutz 1962, 168–169).

Also, in the natural attitude, this world is "my one and unitary, pregiven, world of working" (Schutz 2013, 281). One might say, with Barber, that working is "the bodily engagement with the world in the pursuit of projects" (Barber 2017, 5). It "consists in those bodily actions that overtly gear into the outer world, that extend beyond covert thinking, and that aim at realizing a project. Such actions, in concert with those of other persons, go into making up the 'world of working'" (Barber 2017, 50).

The world of the natural attitude is also a naive one, as far as the subject takes for granted the existence of the world as it is, its social imposed relevances, and everything that goes along with it. In my naive life, "it is self-evident to me that the world actually exists and that it is actually *thus,* as I experience it" (Schutz 1962, 135). "Hence, the naively living person" (that is, the "healthy, grown-up, and wide-awake" human being) "automatically has in hand, so to speak, the meaningful complexes which are valid for him. From things inherited and learned, from the manifold sedimentations of tradition, habituality, and his own previous constitutions of meaning, which can be retained and reactivated, his *stored experience* of his life-world is built up as a closed meaningful complex" (Schutz 1962, 135–136).

So, while living in the natural attitude, we take unquestionably for granted the sociocultural world in which we were born, and we experience it as a pregiven world in which we must find our "bearings" and with which we "have to come to terms" (Schutz 1962, 145). Moreover,

we find ourselves geared into a multiplicity of relations to the phenomena of the social world surrounding us. The social world appears to us as simply given. We simply accept it surrounded by the world of nature without asking about its constitution and without thinking much about how it really comes to pass that we live with others, affect them, are affected [. . .] by them while carrying on our own lives [. . .] we, who simply live straightforwardly, are at the middle of events. Our daily life of work and leisure in planned continuity is, so to speak, the axis around which the social world is grouped in its multiple perspectives. (Schutz 2013, 243–244)

While living in the naivety of the natural attitude, we do not have any motive "to raise the transcendental question concerning the actuality of the world or concerning the reality of the *alter ego,* or to make the jump into the reduced sphere" (Schutz 1962, 135). Rather, we posit "this world in a *general thesis* as meaningfully valid" for us with all that we find in it, "with all natural things, with all living beings (especially with human beings), and with meaningful products of all sorts (tools, symbols, language systems, works of art, etc.)" (Schutz 1962, 135).

Also, the world of the natural attitude is dogmatic because it is, for us, "unquestioned until further notice but may be called into question at any time" (Schutz 1962, 145). This is how Schutz describes this feature of our natural world. Let me quote in extenso from an early draft of the paper "On Multiple Realities":

Characteristically, persons in the natural attitude take the world and its objects for granted until counterproof. As long as the once established schemes of reference work as systems of our warranted experiences, and as long as the actions and operations performed under its guidance yield the desired results, in the natural attitude we are not interested whether this world does "really" exist or whether it is only a coherent system of consistent appearances.

We have no reason to cast doubt either upon our past experiences or upon our senses which, or so we believe, represent things to us as they "really" are. If a new experience pops up and proves to be "strange" and is not subsumable under the existing stock of my previous experiences, or if the inconsistency of such new experiences compels us to revise our former beliefs—these facts do not change anything in the basic fact: while maintaining our natural attitude we take our beliefs for granted unless a specific motivation forces us to "stop and think." (Schutz 1996, 26–27)

Hence, to the natural attitude, "the world we live in is a world of well circumscribed objects with definite qualities [. . . and not] a mere aggregate of colored spots, incoherent noises, centers of warmth and cold" (Schutz 1962, 208, 306), which "are accepted simply as real" (Schutz 1996, 280). Then, "for pragmatic reasons," in the natural attitude "a world of identical objects is assumed as unquestionable and self-evidently given" (Schutz 2011, 228). Accordingly, inconsistencies and incompatibilities of experiences "partaking of the same cognitive style, do not necessarily entail the withdrawal of the accent of reality from the respective province of meaning as a whole but merely the invalidation of the particular experience or experiences within that province" (Schutz 1962, 230).

This unquestioned, taken-for-granted aspect of the natural attitude is per se dogmatic because the objects given to it are not subjected to critique. However, one may also say that it is dogmatic because those who remain in the natural attitude have not yet performed the transcendental phenomenological reduction, in which one is obliged not to take anything for granted. As Barber (2017, 98) notes, one who lives in the natural attitude has not yet performed the phenomenological transcendental *epoché* which frees us "from a naïve absoluteness and from our bondage to that which is familiar (*Bekanntheit*) and accustomed (*Gewohnheit*), as taking off the blindfold that blinds us to the endless wealth of life possibilities, as launching us in a 'radical new direction,' and as enabling us to see the new world of transcendental subjectivity."

In the natural attitude, objects are not for contemplation. They are "objects among which we move, which resist us and upon which we may act" (Schutz 1962, 208, 306). The world experience in the natural attitude "is given to us as the universal persistent ground of being and as the universal field of all of our activities" (Schutz 1966, 107). Therefore, "we have not a theoretical but an eminently practical interest" in it. As we said, this world "is to us not an object of thought but a field of dominations, of action: we may pursue our goals within it; and we have to change it in order to realize our purposes" (Schutz 1996, 26). This means that "the ultimate relevance governing this domain is pragmatic; namely, that I seek to intervene in the world bodily to realize my projects" (Barber 2017, 3).

One of the reasons why we have an eminently practical interest in the world of the natural attitude is "the necessity of complying with the basic requirements of our life" (Schutz 1962, 227; see also Schutz and Luckmann 1989, 306). This is why the world of the natural attitude is not to be contemplated but dominated.

For the above said, "the wide-awake man within the natural attitude is primarily interested in that sector of the world of his everyday life which is within his scope and which is centered in space and time around himself" (Schutz 1962, 222–223). Hence, our own body has a centrality regarding the world of the natural attitude:

I experience the world as organized in space and time around myself as a center. The place my body occupies at a certain moment within this world, my actual "Here," is the starting point from which I take my bearing in space. It is, so to speak, the center "*0*" of a system of coordinates which determines certain dimensions of orientation in the surrounding field and the distances and perspectives of the objects therein: they are above or underneath, before or behind, right or left, nearer or farther. And, in a similar way, my "actual Now" is the origin of all the time-perspectives under which I organize the events within the world, such as the categories of fore and aft, past and future, simultaneity and succession, sooner or later, etc. (Schutz 1962, 306–307)

In accordance with the primacy of the body for its organization, we do not only work within but also upon the world of the natural attitude:

Our bodily movements—kinaesthetic, locomotive, operative—gear, so to speak, into the world, modifying or changing its objects and their mutual relationships. On the other hand, these objects offer resistance to our acts which we have either to overcome or to which we have to yield. [. . .] World, in this sense, is something that we have to modify by our actions or that modifies our actions. (Schutz 1962, 208–209)

This world that we have to modify "is from the outset not the private world of the single individual but an intersubjective world, common to all of us" (Schutz 1962, 208). Within the natural attitude we "experience the Other's self in its unbroken totality," in "the vivid present of the We-relation" (Schutz 1962, 254). In accordance, "the 'We' is given to each of us prior to the sphere of the I [. . .] . If we retain the natural attitude as men among other men, the existence of Others is no more questionable to us than the existence of an outer world" (Schutz 1962, 168).

Actually, in the world of the natural attitude we have direct experience of our fellow men, and we assume that we both perceive the same objects.[4] Therefore, the life-world is an "intersubjective world that existed long before my birth and was experienced and interpreted by others, our predecessors, as an organized world. Now it is given to our experience and requires our interpretation" (Schutz and Luckmann 1989, 293). Briefly, it is "the intersubjective world into which we were born and within which we grew up" (Schutz 1996, 26).

Thus, in the natural attitude, we come upon our fellow men and take their existence for granted just as we take for granted the existence of the natural objects we encounter. Schutz puts this assumption in a short formula that expresses it from the point of view of "the human being who is looking at the world from within the natural attitude [. . .]: The Thou (or other person) is conscious, and his stream of consciousness is temporal in character, exhibiting the same basic form as mine" (Schutz 1962, 98). Furthermore:

> In the natural attitude I take it for granted that fellow-men exist, that they act upon me as I upon them, that—at least to a certain extent—communication and mutual understanding among us can be established, and that this is done with the help of some system of signs and symbols within the frame of some social organization and some social institutions—none of them of my own making. (Schutz 1962, 145)

The signs and symbols we use to interpret the world in the natural attitude compose the stock of knowledge available in our social world, which "existed before we were born; [and] it is given to our experiences and interpretations" (Schutz 1996, 26). Indeed, "we have at our disposal a certain stock of knowledge of this world"—a "stock of acquired experiences [that] functions as our scheme of reference"—which "has been constituted by our own actions of interpretation, by learning from others, by habits formed and traditions handed down from parents and teachers and from teachers of our teachers" (Schutz 1996, 26). Therefore, "all interpretation of this world is based upon a stock of previous experiences of it, [. . .] which in the form of 'knowledge at hand' function as a scheme of reference" (Schutz 1962, 208).

As any ordinary man, in every moment of our lived experience we light upon past experiences in the storehouse of our consciousness. We know about the world, and we know what to expect: "to the natural man all his past experiences are present as *ordered*, as knowledge or as awareness of what to expect, just as the whole external world is present to him as ordered. [. . .] The particular patterns of order we are now considering are synthetic meaning-configurations of already encountered lived experiences" (Schutz 1967, 81). For instance, in the natural attitude we have "experiences of the external world and its objects" (Schutz 1967, 81) which are, from the outset, "experienced in their typicality" (Schutz 1962, 306) and included in "a stock of knowledge of physical things and fellow creatures, of social collectives and of artifacts, including cultural objects" (Schutz 1967, 81).

Schutz calls these patterns "the schemes of our experience" and defines them as "a meaning context which is a configuration of our past experiences embracing conceptually the experiential objects to be found in the latter but not the process by which they were constituted. The constituting process itself is entirely ignored, while the objectivity constituted by it is taken for granted" (Schutz 1967, 81–82).

Last, but not least, the natural attitude is not just a given. One of the most original contributions of Schutz's is to have shown that the natural attitude is itself the product of a peculiar *epoché*. Indeed, this world, which "is accepted without question and just as what it appears to be," which is presupposed "as long as there do not appear motives which run counter to this general sup-position [*Generalansetzung*]" and which we live in "our naive attitude [. . .] presupposing its reality" (Schutz 1996, 111), springs off from our suspension of the doubt that it might be otherwise than just the way we conceive it.

In the natural attitude we "simply accept as facts the phenomena" (Schutz 2013, 225). This means that "as long as the harmony of experiencing does not disintegrate, [. . . we] do not distinguish between seeming and being. In a common sense we can say that also and just in the natural attitude a kind of *epoché* is exercised which is certainly radically distinct in kind from the phenomenological *epoché*" (Schutz 2013, 225).

Unlike the phenomenological *epoché*, whereby we suspend the belief in the reality of the world and its objects, in the *epoché* of the natural attitude we suspend the doubt in its existence. What we put in brackets "is the doubt that the world and its objects might be otherwise than they appear" to us (Schutz and Luckmann 1989, 308; Schutz 1996, 27). Accordingly, if this *epoché* sus-pends doubt itself, then its object is to prevent skepticism:

> In contrast, the phenomenological *epoché,* that directly emerges from the basic skeptical attitude, [the *epoché* of the natural attitude] exercises *epoché* on the affirmation of reality and leaves aside whether what human beings view in real-ity is genuine being or mere illusion.
>
> In this attitude of the natural *epoché*, [. . .] in its manifold of perspectively divided perceptions and apperceptions there is constituted for the self the core of reality of its surrounding world as the world in the range of vision and hearing and reach. (Schutz 2013, 281)

In the natural attitude, I just live amid other human beings and amid objects of the outer world not being aware of myself (Schutz 1962, 168). I am living "in my acts and thoughts, and in doing so, I am exclusively directed towards the objects of my acts and thoughts" (Schutz 1962, 168–169). Nonetheless, even "remaining in the natural attitude, and this means without performing the transcendental reduction, I may always turn in an act of reflection from the objects of my acts and thoughts to my acting and thinking" (Schutz 1962, 169). We may always "stop and think" and thus direct our experience toward the subjectivity constitutive of their objects.

> In doing so, I render my previous acts and thoughts objects of another, the reflective thought by which I grasp them. Then my "Self," which has been hidden as yet by the objects of my acts and thoughts, emerges. It does not merely enter the field of my consciousness in order to appear on its horizon or at its center; rather, it alone constitutes this field of consciousness. Consequently, all the performed acts, thoughts, feelings reveal themselves as originating in *my* previous acting, *my* thinking, *my* feeling. The whole stream of consciousness is through and through the stream of my personal life, and my Self is present in any of my experiences. (Schutz 1962, 169)

Once done that, we can perform the transcendental phenomenological reduction.

THE TRANSCENDENTAL
PHENOMENOLOGICAL REDUCTION

Some phenomenologists consider Schutz an anti-transcendentalist. A few even take this as the hallmark of his view on Husserl.[5] However, Schutz never rejected in toto transcendental phenomenology but only its last step, when the phenomenological ego turns toward the transcendental ego, the pure, absolute I, out of time and therefore lacking every name.[6] Furthermore, Schutz was for long contemplative with these aspects of Husserl's work which sometimes seemed to him an unnecessary complication, a sterile effort, but not a total mistake. Only in his later years did Schutz radicalize his attitude toward Husserl, focusing on the difficulties and deficiencies of the fifth Cartesian Meditation. But even then, he still admitted some aspects of the transcendental phenomenological reduction. What is more, he saw no contradictions between some of its outcomes and worldly phenomenology, given that for transcendental phenomenology, "there is no doubt that the world exists and that it manifests itself in the continuity of harmonious experience as a universe" (Schutz 1962, 115). Consequently, Schutz argues that this certainty must be made intelligible by proving its relativity "to the transcendental subjectivity which alone has the ontic sense of absolute being" (Schutz 1962, 115). In doing so, the philosopher must undertake the "*epoché* or transcendental phenomenological reduction":

> he must deprive the world which formerly, within the natural attitude, was simply posited as being, of just this posited being, and he must return to the living stream of his experiences of the world. In this stream, however, the world is kept exactly with the contents which actually belong to it. With the execution of the *epoché*, [. . .] what is grasped [. . .] is the pure life of consciousness in which and through which the whole objective world exists for me, by virtue of the fact that I experience it, perceive it, remember it, etc. In the *epoché*, however, I abstain from belief in the being of this world, and I direct my view exclusively to my consciousness of the world. (Schutz 1962, 115)

In the natural attitude, we live "*within* the meaning-endowing acts themselves," being "aware only of the objectivity constituted in them." For performing the transcendental phenomenological reduction, we have to turn away from the world of objects in order to direct our gaze at our inner stream of consciousness and bracket the natural world to attend only to our conscious experiences and become aware of the process of constitution (Schutz 1962, 36–37).

Consequently, Schutz admitted that the phenomenological *epoché* "is necessary in order to overcome the natural attitude" (Schutz 1996, 27), in which

> we accept as unquestionable the world of facts which surrounds us as existent out there. To be sure, [in the natural attitude] we might throw doubt upon any *datum* of that world out there, we might even distrust as many of our experiences of this world as we wish; the naive belief in the existence of *some* outer world, this "general thesis of the natural standpoint," will imperturbably subsist. (Schutz 1966, 5)

However, while remaining in the natural attitude, I am not aware that all the objects of my acts and thoughts—not only physical objects but also the ones we call the "Others," the "we" and "you" and "they" and the like, "are relative to my Self and that only my existence within this world as a Self makes this relationship and relativity possible" (Schutz 1962, 168).

According to Schutz, "a truly beginning philosophy must 'refrain' from every judging" about the existence of corporeal nature and the concrete surrounding life-world, "and from every experiential believing in them. It has to 'put out of action' all position-taking toward the pregiven objective world; it has to exercise a '*phenomenological epoché*'" (Schutz 1996, 157). This is how it is done:

by a radical effort of our mind we can alter this attitude [. . .] by suspending belief. We just make up our mind to refrain from any judgment concerning spatiotemporal existence, or in technical language, we set the existence of the world "out of action," we "bracket" our belief in it. But using this particular "*epoché*" we not only "bracket" all the commonsense judgments of our daily life about the world out there, but also all the propositions of the natural sciences which likewise deal with the realities of this world from the natural standpoint. (Schutz 1966, 5)

With the phenomenological *epoché* we bracket the objective world, to which "belong not only transcendent objects [*Objekte*] but also the mundane human ego of the meditating person as something existing in the world and, therefore, as a '*psychological subject*' of inner experience" (Schutz 1996, 157–158). This way we access

> to the pure life of consciousness of the *transcendental ego cogitans* which exists for itself "prior" to all mundane existence as well as to the latter's real mental processes [*reale Erlebnisse*] in and through which mundane existence alone achieves the validity of being. As a result, the questionable assumptions of the existence of the objective world are reduced to the indubitable experiences [*Erlebnisse*] (to the *cogitationes* in the Cartesian sense) of the world by the meditating person. At the same time, the transcendental subjectivity of the cognizing ego is revealed as the originary ground of cognition: in apodictic evidence, but only in the universality of an "open horizon" of the past, of transcendental capacities and habitualities which belong to it. (Schutz 1996, 157)

What remains after performing this bracketing is "the concrete fullness and entirety of the stream of our experience containing all our perceptions, our reflections, in short, our cogitations" (Schutz 1966, 5). However, these cogitations are still intentional ones, and thus "their correlative 'intentional objects' persist also within the brackets" (Schutz 1966, 5); they are not "posited objects" anymore but "just 'appearances,' phenomena, and, as such, rather 'unities' or 'senses' ('meanings'). The method of phenomenological reduction, therefore, makes accessible the stream of consciousness in itself as a realm of its own in its absolutely unique nature" (Schutz 1966, 5–6).

After performing the phenomenological reduction, we can experience our stream of consciousness and describe its inner structure. Once we do that, the ego "as psychological subject, as natural human ego," the ego which belongs to the world subjected to phenomenological reduction, is reduced "by means of the *epoché* to my transcendental-phenomenological experience of self" (Schutz 1996, 157). We say this *epoché* is transcendental "because it exhibits the rigorous correlate to the 'transcendence of everything mundane' and, thereby, also of my mundane ego. This ego receives its sense and its validity of being only from me as the one who meditates philosophically in the reduction" (Schutz 1996, 157–158).

THE EGOLOGICAL REDUCTION

As just seen, what remains once the transcendental reduction has been performed "is nothing less than the universe of our conscious life, the stream of thought in its integrity, with all its activities and with all its cogitations and experiences" (Schutz 1962, 105). By executing the *epoché*, "I reduce the universe of my conscious life to my own transcendental sphere (*transzendentale Eigensphäre*), to my concrete being as a monad" (Schutz 1962, 105). In accordance, the transcendental phenomenological reduction leads to the egological sphere.

Even if Schutz chooses to end the reduction in the concrete ego (in the monad, not in the absolute ego, as Husserl does), he operates within the transcendentally reduced sphere. I will borrow Embree's idea that it is the primordial reduction (which Husserl operates within the egological reduced sphere) "that is opposed [by Schutz], but the egological reduction or something like it nevertheless seems assumed" (Embree 2009a, 211). I would say that Schutz practices a kind of limited transcendentalism, meaning that he does not follow Husserl's transcendental reduction all the way through but only until it discloses the egological sphere, which Schutz conceived as a pre-reflective transcendent stream of consciousness. I will also endorse Embree's remark that Schutz assumed that "the ego or I is something that accompanies the stream of consciousness in an inwardly transcendent way and that reflection discloses as always already and identically there" (Embree 2009a, 240).

Therefore, Schutz holds to the egologically reduced sphere as the ultimate substratum of all phenomenological inquiries. According to Embree (2009b, 181), he even uses the word "egology" in his review of Husserl in the French translation of *Cartesian Meditations* in 1932. There, having dealt with the primordial reduction, the egological reduction "seems assumed as already performed" (Embree 2009b, 183). Yet again in his unpublished papers of 1936–1937, he speaks of "a transcendental or phenomenologizing *ego*" (Schutz 2013, 211), this time in reference to the self and to the transcendental Ego reached through Husserl's transcendental reduction (Schutz 2013, 233). Here, Schutz situates his analysis within "the ego after exercise of the phenomenological reduction" and states that "we are not spared from introducing the realm of the transcendental sphere" (Schutz 2013, 252).

Also in his paper on William James in 1941, Schutz seems to perform the egological reduction although he does not mention egology: he excludes the topic of intersubjectivity to focus on personal consciousness from the perspective of pure psychology (Embree 2009a, 240). Again in his Scheler essay, Schutz seems to operate within the egological reduction (Embree 2009a, 206). The same applies to *Reflections on the Problem of Relevance*, where Schutz relies on the egological reduction (Embree 2009a, 209). Thus, there is plenty of evidence that Schutz considered egology a main aspect of his phenomenology, whether he mentions it or not. The transcendentally reduced egological sphere becomes then a fertile field of research.

THE EIDETIC REDUCTION

Once the egological reduction has been performed, the phenomenologist "aims at dealing with the eidetic of the transcendentally purified conscious-ness, with the pure Ego" (Schutz 1966, 46). To that purpose, he may "perform the transition to the eidetic attitude, abstracting from the existential positing of actual experience and moving in free arbitrariness in the realm of 'empty possibilities'" (Schutz 1966, 43). This is how Schutz considers that we should proceed:

> the process of ideation we put out of play the relationship of our experience with the world and liberate the environmental horizon of the variants from any attachment to any experiential activity. By doing so we place ourselves in a world of pure phantasy, of pure possibilities. Each of them may now become the central member of a set of possible pure variations in the mode of arbitrari-ness; from each of them we may arrive at an absolute pure eidos—provided that the sequences of variations can be connected to a single one. (Schutz 1966, 107–108)

In this view, the phenomenologist "may perform the 'eidetic reduction,' dis-carding all questions as to the actual unities of consciousness, and turn to the eidos of perception, the eternally identical meaning of possible perceptions in general" (Schutz 1962, 44). He can do the same

> with respect to recollections, phantasies, expectations, cognitive, emotional, volitive experiences of any kind. Directed toward the essences in eidetic-intuitive apperception, the full contents of these experiences and their intentional corre-lates, such as they are given to psychological experience are fully preserved in the eidos. (Schutz 1962, 44)

In the eidetic attitude, as a phenomenologist, I am free "to transform this perceived object in my fancy, by successively varying its features" (Schutz 1962, 114). In whatever way I transform "the 'Gestalt' of the thing in free phantasy," vary its qualitative determinations, or change its real properties, all these products of my phantasy "still show particular regularities" (Schutz 1966, 43). I may imagine an infinite number of variations, but they "do not touch on a set of characteristics" which remain "unchanged among all the imagined transformations": its "kernel" or *eidos* (Schutz 1966, 43). "Thus eidetic investigations do not deal with concrete real things but with possibly imaginable things," and "the latter are of even greater importance for the phenomenological approach" than the former (Schutz 1966, 43).

Eidetic investigations not only have to be pursued in order to account for things but also for the psyche, given that the phenomenological reduction "makes accessible the stream of consciousness in itself as a realm of its own in its absolutely unique nature," which can be experienced and whose inner structure can be described (Schutz 1966, 5–6). Phenomenological psychology is the aprioristic science which must carry out this task and deal with the *Eidos*, "with the essence of thoughts" (Schutz 1966, 6). Schutz conceives it as a *psychology of intentionality* and a *constitutive phenomenology of the natural attitude* which must be undertaken as an eidetic mundane science (Schutz 1962, 132).

PHENOMENOLOGICAL PSYCHOLOGY

Now that we are familiar with eidetic phenomenology, we can apply it to the invariant structures of our mind and start doing phenomenological psychology, which turns out to be essential to understand Schutz's work (Yu 2014, 226; see also Yu 2007). By the way, "Schutz seems the first after Husserl to mention the project" of a phenomenological psychology (Embree 2008, 147).

Interesting to note is that, for Schutz, eidetics operates on reflexive analysis, not on reduced phenomena. In other words: phenomenological psychology is reflexive, not strictly phenomenological (see Schutz 1962, 169). The phenomenological reduction comes later and is linked to the transcendental reduction as its prelude. Let us see what it consists of.

According to Schutz, phenomenological psychology must become aprioristic, which means that it "cannot deal with 'matters of fact' [. . .] . It has to deal with the 'Eidos,' with the essence of thoughts and must therefore use *eidetic* methods" (Schutz 1966, 6). In order to do that, we first have to understand "by eidetic description the 'problem of the inner development (*Zeitigung*) of the immanent time sphere,' [then] we can apply our conclusions without risk of error to the phenomena of the natural attitude" as long as we "remain 'on the ground of inner appearance as the appearance of that which is peculiar to the psychic' [. . . in order to seek] the invariant, unique, a priori structure of the mind, in particular of a society composed of living minds" (Schutz 1962, 44).

Thus, in psychological introspection, and still within the sphere of the natural attitude, we can carry on, as a constitutive phenomenology of the natural standpoint, "that phenomenological psychology which, according to Husserl, is, in the final analysis, nothing other than a psychology of pure intersubjectivity" (Schutz 1962, 44). This kind of analysis still works exclusively within the mundane sphere and is "restricted to the constitutional analysis of the natural attitude" (Schutz 1996, 26).

In addition, phenomenological psychology is—in Schutz's view—a science which must be pursued in two different levels, rational and descriptive. In the first place, rational psychology, as a phenomenological "eidetic science of the realm of the psyche" (Schutz 1966, 44) does not deal with empirical facts but with "the correlates of those transcendental constitutional phenomena which are related to the natural attitude. Consequently, it has to examine the invariant, peculiar, and essential structures of the mind" (i.e., their a priori structures) (Schutz 1962, 132) and, based on them, "the aprioristic structures of the social sciences" by means of intentional analysis (Schutz 1966, 164). In the second place, descriptive psychology deals with "the concrete description of the spheres of consciousness [. . .] within the natural attitude" (Schutz 1966, 132). It consists in "the description of a closed sphere of the intentionalities [. . . which] requires not only a concrete description of the experiences of consciousness [. . .] but also necessarily the description of the conscious (intentional) 'objects in their objective sense' found in active inner experiences" (Schutz 1966, 132).

Briefly, phenomenological psychology is not only an eidetic but also a descriptive science (Schutz 1966, 7). Thus, to a certain extent, phenomenological psychology is a "'positive' science promoted in the 'natural attitude' with the world before it as the basis for all its themes" (Schutz 1966, 7). It is a science of the conception of the world valid for "the naively living human being" (Schutz 1962, 127).

PHENOMENOLOGICAL PSYCHOLOGY AND TRANSCENDENTAL REDUCTION

Phenomenological psychology is pursued in the constitutional process in the inner time consciousness within the phenomenological reduction, but only insofar as it is needed to clearly understand this inner time consciousness (Schutz 1967, 43). Once we understand the problem of the inner development of the inner time field by means of the eidetic reduction, we can safely apply our conclusions to phenomena of the natural attitude, on one condition: that we stay as phenomenological psychologists, in the realm of the inner appearance as the manifestation of what is peculiar to the psychic. Schutz does not propose a science of facts in this internal realm of appearance but a science of essences in search of the invariably unique a priori structure of the mind (Schutz 1967, 44). However, no revisions of the conclusions regarding inner time need to be made to apply them to the realm of ordinary life since every analysis made in the phenomenological reduction is also valid within the psychological introspection, therefore within the natural attitude (Schutz 1967, 44). Accordingly,

the transcendental reduction is important for phenomenological descriptive psychology not only because it reveals the stream of consciousness and its features in their purity, but, above all, because some very important structures of consciousness can be made visible only within this reduced sphere. Since to each empirical determination within the phenomenological reduction there necessarily corresponds a parallel feature within the natural sphere and vice versa, we can always turn back to the natural attitude and there make use of all the insights we have won within the reduced sphere. (Schutz 1966, 6)[7]

Hence, for Schutz, counter to what Husserl holds, the transcendental attitude must be reconducted to the natural attitude, not the other way around.

PHENOMENOLOGICAL ONTOLOGY
AND THE SCIENCES

Phenomenology is significant not only for the social and cultural sciences, but also for all kinds of sciences. Schutz claims that "the results of phenomenological research cannot and must not clash with the tested results of the mundane sciences, or even with the proved doctrines of so-called philosophies of the sciences" (Schutz 1967, 115). He mentions two good reasons for this.

On the one hand, the method of empirical sciences leans on phenomenological ontology because it is "determined or at least co-determined by the general essential structure of the realm of reality to which these sciences refer" (Schutz 1966, 42). Thus, "the examination of this structure as to its constitution in pure intuition" should lead to "an ontology of this particular realm" (Schutz 1966, 42). Consequently, ontology should refer to "the various regions of objectivities and to the methods which any empirical science dealing with facts belonging to these regions has to observe" (Schutz 1966, 42). Therefore, "there must *a priori* exist as many ontologies as there are regional concepts and, consequently, all radical classifications of the sciences depend upon the concept of the 'region' [. . .] and its essence which can be disclosed by noematic intuition" (Schutz 1966, 42–43). This is one reason why phenomenological research cannot clash with mundane sciences:

because it co-determines (by saying the least) the *eidos* of the objects which mundane sciences take for granted.

On the other hand, a clash is impossible because "the clarification of the ontologies has to precede that of the pertinent empirical sciences" (Schutz 1966, 48). Accordingly, for Schutz, "it is the ideal of phenomenology to establish a complete realm of fully clarified ideas, that is, a complete system of all intuitively knowable essences" (Schutz 1966, 48) by means of eidetic analysis both in the mundane and the reduced sphere (Schutz 1962, 113). Such clarification of ideas is to be found in the "original method" of eidetic investigation, which "opens the way to a scientific ontology" (Schutz 1962, 113). Indeed, "only by the eidetical method may we [. . .] discover and describe the important relationship of foundation which subsists between certain ontological realms" (Schutz 1962, 113). This is why Schutz, in a Husserlian spirit, states that "phenomenology has its field of research in its own right, and hopes to end where the others begin" (Schutz 1962, 113).

As a consequence, the relation of phenomenology to the social sciences cannot be demonstrated by merely "analyzing concrete problems of sociology or economics [. . .] with phenomenological methods" (Schutz 1962, 116), among other reasons because there are questions that cannot be answered by the methods of the social sciences but require a philosophical analysis (Schutz 1962, 117) since the discoveries of all empirical sciences "take place within the frame of an *a priori*, which cannot be grasped by the dogmatic empirical sciences but is accessible to the eidetic methods of phenomenology" (Schutz 1966, 42). So even if phenomenological methods can be "applied with the greatest success within the empirical sphere [. . .] only by recourse to the eidetical sphere can the aprioristic character of phenomenology as a *prima philosophia* and even as a phenomenological psychology be assured" (Schutz 1962, 113).

It is important to notice that, while Schutz admitted the legitimacy of first philosophy, his work was mainly devoted to technical problems posed by the social and cultural sciences. However, he dealt with central issues of *prima philosophia* such as "reality"—a main concern in many of his writings. In his latest years, he also addressed the *humana conditio* from the perspective of philosophical anthropology. However, some important problems of first philosophy remained undiscussed. Especially important is the question of givenness, which is the basis of his position on intersubjectivity and of what some consider to be a "given ontology" of everyday life-world (López Saenz 1995, 71). Probably Schutz intended to address these matters in the future since he was increasingly interested in fundamental questions regarding the human condition. Unfortunately, he did not make it explicit, so the question remains open to interpretation.

ON ABSOLUTE CERTAINTY: AN EPILOGUE
ON NATURALIZED PHENOMENOLOGY

To summarize, we can say that, for Schutz, phenomenology is a technical task consisting in the clarification of sense and meaning structures of the natural attitude, both in its noematic and its noetic poles. This duty can be undertaken in three different levels: transcendental, eidetic, empirical. This means that, although transcendental phenomenology is a "legitimate task" for philosophy, it is not needed in empirical sciences because they are not founded on transcendental philosophy but in everyday thinking and acting (Yu 2007, 760).

Consequently, empirical sciences are based on the life-world and not on any particular philosophy. Of course, it is possible to undertake a philosophical exploration of the life-world, but this "paramount reality" remains open to different approaches. For instance, it is accessible to a psychology of the natural attitude and even (in Schutz's latest writings) to a psychiatry of the "normal natural attitude" (see Schutz 1962, 260–286). Accordingly, transcendental phenomenology is just one of many different possible explorations of the life-world. This explains why "Schutz felt no need in his own investigations for transcendental reduction and considered 'phenomenological psychology' or 'constitutive phenomenology of the natural attitude' sufficient for his purposes" (Embree 2009a, 184).

In this regard, we can see in Schutz a non-cognitivist naturalization of phenomenology which makes his stance amazingly current. At a time when writers like Shaun Gallagher, Dan Zahavi, and others have achieved great success discoursing on this matter, the productiveness of the Schutzian perspective has not yet been fully noticed, perhaps because it challenges the very premises of the cognitivist approach by rejecting scientism and going beyond intellectualist conceptions of intersubjectivity.

In addition, Schutz conceives his naturalist program between two fronts: on the one hand, orthodox phenomenologists who saw nothing deep or lasting in the natural attitude; on the other hand, those who capitulate to objectivist naturalist scientism and positivist science, reluctant to any *sui generis* manifestations of the life of spirit (*Geist*).

This Solomonic position is adequately described by Vaitkus, who distinguishes Schutz's natural attitude from those assumed by the average phenomenologist and by the natural scientist. Most phenomenologists (in particular, philosophical phenomenologists) consider the natural attitude "as merely a first methodological level or step on the way towards much deeper phenomenological analyses" (Vaitkus 2005, 98). And most natural scientists take "naturality" or "naturalism" as related to their own empirical sciences. For Schutz, instead, naturality "is not to be confused with any sort of naturalism or concept of nature from the natural sciences but is to be understood in a much deeper lived sense and precisely in relationship to the above potentially developing direction taken by transcendental phenomenology" (Vaitkus 2005, 104). What Schutz conceived as "naturalism" is the description of the constitutive mechanism of our natural attitude in the life-world. He considered that "the notions of life-world and natural attitude are inseparably bound up together" (Yu 2007, 761) because the natural attitude is worldly oriented.

In consequence, the phenomenologist, as well as the layman and the scientist, take as the starting point the world in which they live, act, and think. We may say, then, that the life-world is the alpha and the omega for any kind of activity: acting and practical thinking, eidetic and empirical science, and transcendental philosophy. No matter what the goal of our reflection is, we should always start by, and end up getting back to, the life-world as the ground of all certainty. Therefore, unlike Husserl, Schutz finds the certainty in the universal structures of our mind and in the anthropological invariable features of the life-world, not necessarily in the transcendental sphere.

This change of perspective produces not only a methodological redefinition whereby the constitutive phenomenology of the natural attitude partially substitutes transcendental phenomenology, but also a renewal of the ontology of the life-world which is no longer seen as merely relative but as endowed with universal and eidetic features that give it a dimension of necessity. Of course, we speak here of mundane (not transcendental) certainty, anchored in the natural attitude, which bestows the Schutzian conception of the life-world with unparalleled originality.

NOTES

1. In a previous paper (Belvedere 2013a), I addressed the larger issue of "What is Schutzian phenomenology?" Here, instead, I will focus on its implications for phenomenological science in general, and for phenomenological sociology in particular.

2. As it is well known, Heidegger called to "free ourselves from the technical interpretation of thinking" and to abandon the idea that philosophy has to "justify" its existence by "elevating itself to the rank of a science" (Heidegger 1998, 240). "The rigor of thinking, in contrast to that of the sciences, does not consist merely in an artificial, that is, technical-theoretical exactness of concepts. It lies in the fact that saying remains purely in the element of the truth of being and lets the simplicity of its manifold dimensions rule" (Heidegger 1998, 240). It is my opinion that Schutz's idea of phenomenology, regarding its method and relation to the sciences, is in clear opposition to Heidegger.

3. On Schutz and the cultural sciences, see Embree (2015).

4. "I thus presuppose that at any given time we are both referring to the same objects, which transcend the subjective experience of either of us. This is so at least

in the world of the natural attitude, the world of everyday life in which one has direct experience of one's fellow men, the world in which I assume that you are seeing the same table I am seeing" (Schutz 1962, 105).

5. See, for instance, López Sáenz (1995, 60). Hindess (2006) also highlights this aspect of Schutz's work. Probably, because Schutz's criticism of Husserlian transcendental phenomenology was so exacting regarding intersubjectivity, it eclipsed other aspects. My aim here is to retrieve some of the numerous concessions that Schutz made to transcendental phenomenology, which have been systematically overlooked by his critics.

6. It could be said that Schutz follows Husserl's lessons *On the Phenomenology of the Consciousness of Internal Time* (Husserl 1991) only regarding the description of the phenomenological time, not regarding the pure ego.

7. This parallelism aims to fluently articulate scientific research and phenomenology rather than clearly separate them like Luckmann does with his idea of a "parallel action": "Luckmann draws a division line between phenomenology and sociology; for him phenomenology is philosophy and sociology is science. The perspective of phenomenology is egological, that of science cosmological; the method of phenomenology is reflective, that of social science inductive. Therefore, the aim of phenomenology is to describe the universal structures of subjective orientation in the world, whereas science aims at explaining the general features of the objective world" (Dreher 2012, 154).

Chapter Two

The Subject Matter of Phenomenological Sociology

What is the subject matter of phenomenological sociology? Does it have a specific realm of objects? Or it is just another way to practice straight and simple sociology?

Ever since Durkheim, sociologists have been told that their discipline has a specific object. It has become customary to introduce sociology by presenting its own, peculiar object. In this view, if our aim is to champion the idea that phenomenological sociology is a science in its own right, we might be expected to provide at least a preliminary description of its specific object. That is exactly the aim of this chapter.

Two underlying assumptions regarding this issue can be observed in the debate presented in the introduction. On one hand, those advocating the idea that phenomenology is a protosociology might be willing to admit that its subject matter is no different from that of mainstream sociology. It just has a distinctive approach to it—eidetic, not empirical. On the other hand, those advocating the idea that it does exist—a phenomenological perspective in sociology might be convinced that its subject matter, object, and methods clearly differ from those of mainstream sociology. This is the view I will support, with the help of Max Scheler, Alfred Schutz, George Psathas, and other distinguished phenomenological sociologists.

We, practitioners of phenomenological sociology, tend to agree with Psathas, who demonstrated that the phenomenological approach is "a new paradigm that offers an alternative to the restricted potential of positivist perspectives" and can offer "a fresh, open, and innovative approach [. . .] avoiding preconceived sociological notions and concepts as well as the established recipes and formulas of research procedures" (Eberle 2012, 139). In other words, for us, phenomenological sociology is a new paradigm and an alternative to positivism. Also Waksler's (1969) claims that phenomenological sociology "works with different assumptions than positivist science," and that "it questions implicit assumptions about reality and knowledge with which sociologists operate" (Eberle 2012, 143). Thus, its goal is not just to provide a philosophical foundation of the social sciences but also to search for new sociological insights.

Accordingly, phenomenological sociology should have a peculiar, specific object of its own. In the following, I will argue that this discipline deals with group phenomena constituted in the natural attitude, addressed not as objects intended by single individuals but by them as members of groups. Seen this way, phenomenological sociology can be defined as a science of the natural attitude of groups.

A SCIENCE OF THE NATURAL ATTITUDE OF GROUPS

The subject matter of phenomenological sociology is the natural attitude of groups. For some scholars, this might come as a surprise for two reasons: one, because there is a widespread consensus that phenomenological sociology—especially as conceived in the Schutzian tradition—deals with the subjective experience of individuals; another, because most phenomenologists deal with the natural attitude from the first person's perspective singular—i.e., from the individual's point of view. However, that was not Schutz's final word on this, and certainly is not my claim here.

I will borrow Embree's enthusiastic support of the first person plural perspective.[1] This was a long-held conviction which he came to express eloquently in his paper at the 41st Annual Meeting of the Husserl Circle, where he said: "One [. . .] often hears it put these days that phenomenology relies on the 'first person perspective,' but one should then ask whether this terminology adapted from linguistics needs to be qualified as 'singular' or 'plural'" (Embree 2010, 40). The idea that phenomenology should begin in the first person singular seemed to be a result of an Eurocentric "knee jerk individualism":

> it had been taken for granted that one begins in the first person singular and assumes that the individual was a concretum. This "knee jerk individual-ism," as I am tempted to call it, seems part of Eurocentrism in contrast with the alleged tendency in East Asian cultures to consider persons as always already members of groups. (Embree 2010, 41)

Embree confronted this egological individualism with a different perspec-tive which he attributed to Schutz although it was indisputably his own. Based on the Schutzian dictum that "we must start from intersubjectivity," he upheld that phenomenology should always begin "in the first person plural perspective" (Embree 2010, 40).

In this line of argument, I will claim that phenomenological sociology deals with group phenomena deeply rooted in the natural attitude. This implies that, since we are already members of some group before we can even conceive ourselves as individuals, the natural attitude is eminently social. And that is exactly the subject matter of phenomenological sociology.

Schutz borrowed from Scheler the idea of a "relative natural conception of the world," which plays a main role in defining the task of the sociology of knowledge. With these terms Scheler referred to "how different things are taken for granted in various historical periods in various situations" (Schutz 2010, 92). The sociologist of knowledge—or, in our view, the phenomeno-logical sociologist—"should also consider situations where what is taken for granted is questioned, where the whole relative natural conception of the world is questioned" (Schutz 2010, 92). Briefly said, sociology of knowl-edge deals with "the underlying relative natural conception of the world" of a group of people, with "their common, unquestioned beliefs, attitudes and forms of behavior" (Schutz 2010, 64).

This "conception is 'natural' because it is largely taken for granted, as a matter of course, without question" (Schutz 2010, 64). In other words, the relative natural conception of the world has to do with our accepting or taking for granted the world we live in, which "may involve a certain 'world-view,' a comprehensive behavior and understanding" (Schutz 2010, 64).

Indeed, the relatively natural worldview prevailing in a social group "is accepted by its members as the only right, good, and efficient way of life. [. . . It] is taken for granted beyond question by the respective social group and thus accepted as socially approved" (Schutz and Luckmann 1989, 288). Also, the relative natural conception of the world predetermines what features of the world "are worthy of being expressed, and therewith what qualities of these features and what relations among them deserve attention, and what typifications, conceptualizations, abstractions, generalizations, and idealiza-tions are relevant for achieving typical results by typical means" (Schutz and Luckmann 1989, 288).

PHENOMENOLOGICAL SOCIOLOGY AS
A GROUP-ORIENTED SCIENCE

Schutz's interest in group phenomena shows that he is not as individualist as most phenomenological sociologists, and even their adversaries, usu-ally think. See, for instance, Overgaard and Zahavi (2009, 101), who claim that the "primary object" of phenomenological sociology is "interpreting," "acting and experiencing individuals." Counter to this kind of reading[2]—mostly inspired in his early writings—Schutz considered (in his latest years) that the "We" is primordial regarding the "I."

> "We" is still something more than a collection or aggregate of Egos (as in, "We, the People"). "We" is not expressive of Ego plus Ego, but instead of Ego plus he, Ego plus thou, etc., and yet is also a unity over and above the plurality of elements constituting it. The peculiarity here is that the items, constituting the unity of We are utterly heterogeneous, rather than homogeneous as in this house plus this house plus this house. (Schutz 2010, 74)

In addition, the We-relationship is to be "the foundation for all other categories of human existence" (Schutz 2010, 44) including the self, the ego, and the like. All of them "are founded on the primal experience of the we-relationship" (Schutz 2010, 44). Thus,

> while one might think that Schutz considers the individuals to be concreta out of which various collective are assembles, his position is actually the opposite. The individual is an abstractum abstracted from concrete collective life and, it would follow, the structure of the social world as a structure of individuals rest on an abstraction and is thus abstract. (Embree 2015, 125–126)

Indeed, Schutz considered a "fictitious abstraction," the idea that individuals may exist separated one from the other: "groups are concrete and individuals considered apart from their memberships are abstractions" (Embree 2015, 43) because *we always already are members of some groups or others. And this is something not always clear in the social world merely considered a structure of individuals*" (Embree 2015, 125, Embree's emphasis).

Hence, the sociohistorical world cannot be understood as a mere structure of individuals because it contains groups that are related one to another in diverse ways. Furthermore, groups are fundamental, regarding individuals, because they are concrete, not abstract:

> metaphorically speaking, groups can "live" and "be born" as well as "die," the analogy between the sociocultural world as a structure of abstract individuals and as a structure of concrete groups holds and can be considered Schutzian in spirit even if somewhat beyond his letter. Moreover, while the social world as a structure of individuals emphasized by Schutz is based on an abstraction, one in which a member's group memberships are abstracted from, the structure of groups in collective life is concrete and thus fundamental. It may even be considered to be what needs ultimately to be clarified beginning from abstracted individuals. (Embree 2015, 129; see also Embree 2011, 11)

The above said clearly indicates that phenomenological sociology does not abide by methodological individualism. However, it does not assume a holistic perspective either. Sure, it deals with collective subjects, but not in a hypostasized, mystified manner. Groups are not impersonal, self-sufficient entities but concrete, real conglomerates of individuals with a life of their own, with their subjective experiences and established meanings. Seen this way,

one can wonder if a group of some sort can serve as a collective subject and function like the self in the structure of individuals and one can also wonder if groups of others can then be related to by such a "subject" in ways analogous to how individual consociates, contemporaries, predecessors, and successors are related to by an individual self. (Embree 2015, 124. See also Embree 2011n3)

If we grant this, then we should also admit that "members of groups can share or hold subjective meanings in common" and can also hold objective meanings (Embree 2015, 125; see also Embree 2011, 4), all of which constitute a We-relation.

This is easier to see in the case of primary groups, which are "consocial collectivities" (Embree 2015, 127). Probably for that reason they allow Embree to elaborate his analogy between the social structure of individuals and that of groups as follows:

when meeting face-to-face, a group of consociates can be analogous to the I or self in the social structure of individuals. One might then speak of this subject as a "We." Such an actualized primary group would then have the collective standpoint from which there could most originally be shared meanings or interpretations, self-interpretations included, from which inwardly as well as outwardly directed influence can be exercised. [. . .] "Thou groups" (not Schutz's expression), might be analogous to the individual consociates in the structure of individuals. After all, such other primary groups can have their own collective internal lives of mutual understanding and interaction when members meet, each group has a common situation that it defines and interprets, these common situations have then shared subjective meanings, and such groups are furthermore both in-groups in relation to other groups as out-groups and vice versa, i.e., We-groups and They-groups, Thou-groups included. [. . .] a group of others thus has its actual or potential collective internal life. (Embree 2015, 127; see also Embree 2011, 7)

It follows that the concrete subject of the social world is the collective life of groups. For that reason, the social world is in the first place a structure of groups which hold their peculiar collective standpoint and (metaphorically speaking) lead their lives in mutual understanding and interaction.

Accordingly, phenomenological sociology does not deal with individuals but with groups. As I indicated before, it focuses on group phenomena. According to Schutz, the sociologist has the duty to "refer to the relationship of the individual within the social group and of social groups with other groups" (Schutz 2011, 275). This means that every group has its internal structure and its external relations with other groups.

Regarding the internal structure of groups, Schutz mentions that "in every group there are systems of kinship, age groups, sex groups, differentiations according to occupations (professions), organizations of power and command, leaders and followers, and thus coherent articulations (gradations) of status and prestige" (Schutz and Luckmann 1989, 278).

Regarding the external relations between groups, Schutz claims that they do not exist isolated. For example, "my clan refers to other clans, my tribe to other tribes, and these are enemies or friends, speaking the same or another language, but they are always organized in their particular social form and display a particular life-style" (Schutz and Luckmann 1989, 277). Hence, there are group relations mediated by the "dialectic of the subjective and objective meanings"—for instance, there are relations between the in-group and the out-group (Schutz 1964, 276) which are always a part of "the life-worldly social world as taken for granted," where everyone who is one of us shares our expressive and interpretative schemes (Schutz and Luckmann 1989, 194). I suggest that also social stratification and social control, social class (Schutz 2011, 277), and similar issues can be, though, in a Schutzian perspective, as forms of group relations.

COLLECTIVE CONSCIOUSNESS
AND SOCIAL CONSTRAINT

Groups are—for Schutz—"a product of social interrelationships and social institutions and structures" (Schutz 2010, 63). By this he means—with a Durkheimian air,[3] "that there is something like a 'social consciousness' at work in the human world" (Schutz 2010, 63), and that phenomena such as speaking can be thought of as "the product of a 'collective consciousness'; more particular, [. . . as] the affirmation of the person within the collective consciousness constituting the given sociality in which a person lives" (Schutz 2010, 70).

In Schutz's view, the notion of collective consciousness is convergent with Scheler's relative natural conception of the world. This is easily noted in phenomena such as *la langue* (as depicted by De Saussure), which is—according to Schutz—a product of *la conscience collective,* not of the individual speaker, because it constrains us to speak in a certain way and forces us to obey grammatical and linguistic laws. Briefly, language is a group phenomenon.

Also Husserl speaks about a collective consciousness. For instance, in *Ideas II*, while referring to social subjectivities as conglomerates of subjects communicatively constituted (Husserl 2005, 242), which presuppose empathy since they are based on an experience of other subjects and of their inner lives (Husserl 2005, 245), he claims that a collectivity as such not only has a consciousness but it might even have a genuine "self-consciousness" if disposed to direct its will toward itself, that is, to auto-configure. Briefly, the idea of a collective consciousness seems to be implied in Husserl's conception of social life and to have similar consequences for an understanding of the realm of social things as in Durkheim.[4]

However, "consciousness" is "the most neglected theoretical term in Durkheim's thought" (Stedman Jones 2007, 98) despite its centrality—i.e., despite the fact that it is "closely tied" in with Durkheim's fundamental concepts" (Stedman Jones 2007, 95). Given its centrality, to clarify what Durkheim meant by "consciousness" is a *conditio* sine qua non for understanding the phenomenological meaning of his sociology.

The first thing to notice is that, for Durkheim, consciousness is related to representations. This, in turn, involves "both the mode of thinking and that which is thought" (Stedman Jones 2003, 18).[5] That is exactly what Husserl called intentionality: the correlation of the *cogito* and the *cogitatum*.[6] So, representations are twofold realities, objective as well as subjective, which are referred to one another. Put otherwise, representations are intentional.

Durkheim's notion of consciousness not only involves intentionality but also what Husserl (1982, 39) called "the primal form belonging to consciousness," which is synthesis. One can find this line of argument, for instance, in *Sociologie et philosophie*, where Durkheim claims that collective consciousness emerges from a synthesis originating in the relations among individual consciousnesses (Durkheim 2004b, 133). Indeed, for him, social syntheses are constituted in "one of the functions of *conscience*," which is "to relate" (Stedman Jones 2007, 99; see also Durkheim 2004a, 133).

Back to Schutz and phenomenological sociology, if there is a social consciousness, there must be some coercion, since for Durkheim (1999, 11) social facts are known for their coercive power. Schutz actually refers "the problem of social coercion" to the notion of "constraint in Durkheim" and to some aspects of Ortega y Gasset's philosophy such as his meditation on greeting, custom, and habit (Schutz and Luckmann 1989, 213, 265). Of particular importance here is Ortega's concept of "*vigencia*," which Schutz calls "enforced presentation." *Vigencia* is "a verbal usage having a coercive life of its own to which we must conform" (Schutz 2010, 92).

Coercive life can take different forms. Schutz mentions *inter alia* socioeconomic determination (Schutz 2011, 94), political predominance and domination, social stratification, and class stratification (Schutz 2010, 65, 94, 99; Schutz and Luckmann 1989, 202). All these subjects are related to what, for Schutz, is the "central concept" (Schutz 1996, 76) and the "fundamental problem of sociology": the problem of relevance (Schutz 1996, 3). Main issues such as social relations and social roles are grounded on "the overlapping or sameness of the participant's systems of relevances" (Schutz 1996, 223).

RELEVANCE AS THE CENTRAL CONCEPT
IN PHENOMENOLOGICAL SOCIOLOGY

It has been said that "relevance" is one of the main sociological concepts in the oeuvre of Schutz. This is only partly true. The whole truth is that "relevance" is the most important concept of all.[7]

Indeed, "relevance" is the core concept in Schutzian phenomenology since every other notion is, one way or another, related to it. Concepts such as natural attitude, finite provinces of meaning, typifications, motives of action, and many others, are based on one kind of relevance or another. And it is not only a sociological concept but a philosophical one as well. Specifically, "relevance" is a description of what consciousness is.

In a way, Cox (1978, viii) is right when he claims that "Schutz's approach to these issues [. . .] must be treated as a contribution to eidetic phenomenology"; in another, he falls short: Schutz's concept of relevance is an approach to intentionality in full,[8] not only to noematic structures but also to noetic acts and, moreover, to the noematic-noetic correlation.

However, Schutz addresses intentionality in the wider context of the field of consciousness. For Schutz, consciousness is not only the inner flow of experience nor the structures of the external world by themselves but a dynamic field where those pre-given structures are attended or unattended according to the mind's selective activity. For sure intentionality is the common thread of Schutz's analysis of relevances, but noetic acts are oriented to *noemata* pertaining to systems of relevances which involve dynamic interrelations with other *noemata*, and relevance systems might evolve into habitual acquisitions of the ego. What is more, the field of consciousness is structured in direct relation to situations endowed with intersubjective as well as objective meanings.[9]

More specifically, relevance is a "basic phenomenon" related to the mind's selective activity (Schutz 2011, 99) that "establishes merely a correlation between two terms having reciprocal import as regards one another" (Schutz 2011, 120). It has to do with the structuration of the field of consciousness "into a thematic kernel which stands out over against a surrounding horizon and is given at any 'now' of inner duration" (Schutz 2011, 95).

Schutz illustrates this with the phenomenon of music, where there is a "relationship between two independent themes simultaneously going on in the same flux or flow" (Schutz 2011, 99). Schutz calls this kind of relationship "counterpoint."

The "counterpointal structure of our mind" is our capacity to hold two themes in grip, "in virtue of which we are able to pursue, like the listener of a piece of polyphonic music, two independent themes simultaneously going on in the same flux, taking one as the focal center and the other as marginal, and vice versa" (Schutz 2011, 160–161). In counterpoint, "the listener's mind may pursue one theme or the other, take one as the main theme and the other as the subordinate one, or vice versa: one determines the other, and nevertheless it remains predominant in the intricate web of the whole structure" (Schutz 2011, 99).

Schutz then makes an analogy between the counterpointal structure of music and what he calls the "counterpointal structure of our personality," which he presents as the "corolary" of "the schizophrenic hypothesis of the ego—namely the fact that in order to make something thematic and another thing horizontal we have to assume an artificial split of the unity of our personality" (Schutz 2011, 99) so that "we are involved in the one actual and the many marginal topical relevances with layers of our personality on different levels of depth" (Schutz 2011, 160–161).

Establishing which theme will be pursued as the main one and which will be subordinated is something proper of the mind's selective activity, which is "simply the title for a set of problems more complicated even than those of field, theme, and horizon—namely, a title for the basic phenomenon we suggest calling relevance" (Schutz 2011, 99).

Within this frame, Schutz depicts "the counterpointal structure of our personality and our stream of consciousness itself" in the following words:

> Living *simultaneously* in various realms of reality, in various tensions of consciousness and modes of *attention à la vie*, in various dimensions of time, putting into play different levels of our personality (or different degrees of anonymity and intimacy), the counterpointal articulation of the themes and horizons pertaining to each of such levels (including finally the schizophrenic patterns of the ego) are all *expressions of the single basic phenomenon: the interplay of relevance structures.* (Schutz 2011, 100–101, Schutz's emphasis)

The relevant "elements" of any system of relevance are the result of "the sedimentation of previous experiences" (Schutz 2011, 150). Schutz then notes that we have to be careful not to be misled by the necessarily static description of this genetic process into interpreting the relegation of the interrupted topic into the margin and the resumption of it as experiences which necessarily stand out in the ongoing flux of our conscious life segregated from all other experiences. Actual and marginal topics are copresent to our mind; they are simultaneous. (Schutz 2011, 160–161)

If a given structure of relevances remains over time, habitualities are likely to develop. In Schutz's words:

If a permanent organization of mental life on various levels or depths occurs in such a manner that the mental activities are subsumed under systems of alternating actual and marginal relevances, then certain habitual possessions of knowledge emerge. Not only does the movement from one to another level become a matter of course (done without question), but as well the system of relevances particular to each set of activities becomes a habitual possession of unquestioned, taken for granted knowledge—unquestioned, however, only within the frame of this particular system of relevances. (Schutz 2011, 161)

Consequently, a given system of relevances is likely to result from a genetic process of sedimentation and habitualization—of institutionalization, even— not just from a single act of attention. In addition, this process involves an objectivation of human activity, which is produced by a consciousness that retains part of our experience "as recognizable and memorable entities" that is then sedimented (Berger and Luckmann 1966, 67).

In addition to this kind of sedimentation, operated by an individual consciousness, intersubjective sedimentation occurs "when several individuals share a common biography, experiences of which become incorporated in a common stock of knowledge" (Berger and Luckmann 1966, 67). In this view, one may say that those individuals have in common a given culture, which is "objective in that it may be experienced and apprehended, as it were, in company. Culture is *there for everybody.* This means that the objects of culture [. . .] may be shared with others. This distinguishes them sharply from any constructions of the subjective consciousness of the solitary individual" (Berger 2011, 17, Berger's emphasis).

One key factor in turning the process of intersubjective sedimentation into a process of social sedimentation is its objectivation in a sign system. It is there that "the possibility of reiterated objectification of the shared experiences arises" (Berger and Luckmann 1966, 67), which makes it "likely that these experiences will be transmitted from one generation to the next, and from one collectivity to another" (Berger and Luckmann 1966, 68).

With objectivation in "an objectively available sign system," a transformation occurs in the sedimented experience. It acquires "a status of incipient

anonymity" by being detached "from their original context of concrete individual biographies" and become "generally available to all who share, or may
share in the future, in the sign system in question" (Berger and Luckmann
1966, 68). This way, experiences become easier to transmit.

Even if any sign system would do, usually the linguistic system is
the decisive.

> Language objectivates the shared experiences and makes them available to all
> within the linguistic community, thus becoming both the basis and the instru-
> ment of the collective stock of knowledge. Furthermore, language provides the
> means for objectifying new experiences, allowing their incorporation into the
> already existing stock of knowledge, and it is the most important means by
> which the objectivated and objectified sedimentations are transmitted in the
> tradition of the collectivity in question. (Berger and Luckmann 1966, 68)

As a consequence of its sedimentation, its designation and transmission
in a linguistic system, experience becomes accessible for those who never
had it before, since linguistic designation "abstracts the experience from
its individual biographical occurrences" and turns it into "an objective possibility for everyone" (Berger and Luckmann 1966, 68). This means that it
becomes anonymous and integrates the common stock of knowledge. Thus,
through objectivation, experience "becomes an objective possibility for
everyone" (Berger and Luckmann 1966, 68) that can be incorporated to a
larger tradition. It can also be taught to new generations and even be diffused
in collectivities totally different from the one in which this experience was
generated and originally transmitted. "Language becomes the depository of
a large aggregate of collective sedimentations, which can be acquired monothetically, that is, as cohesive wholes and without reconstructing their original
process of formation" since "the actual origin of the sedimentations" becomes
"unimportant" (Berger and Luckmann 1966, 69).

As we were saying, social sedimentation is transmitted from one generation to another through socialization. This occurs amid a system of relevances
through which groups establish what features of their life-worlds are worthy
of being expressed, and what typifications, conceptualizations, abstractions,
generalizations, and idealizations are relevant for achieving typical results by
typical means and, consequently, must be incorporated by the individual for
him to become a competent member of the group.

According to Schutz, there are three types of relevances: topic, interpretive, motivational. Each of them can be either "intrinsic" or "imposed." In
addition, "there are not such things as isolated relevances. Whatever their
type, they are always interconnected and grouped together in systems"

(Schutz 2011, 117); "they appear in the form of systems, of 'chains' interconnected with one another" (Schutz 2011, 122).

Intrinsic topic relevances are "those by virtue of which something is constituted as problematic in the midst of the unstructuralized field of unprob-
lematic familiarity—and therewith the field into theme and horizon" (Schutz
2011, 107). Intrinsic topic relevances are those in which "we may voluntarily
structure a field into thematic kernel and horizontal background, and we may
even by means of such an act determine the field itself as well as its limits"
(Schutz 2011, 109). Instead, imposed topic relevances are those in which we
cannot determine this field voluntarily (Schutz 2011, 108) but it is "imposed
by means of *social* interaction determined by the acts of our fellowmen or
our own as individuals or social groups" (Schutz 2011, 109). Interpretive
relevances, in turn, have "*a curious double function.*"

> *Not only is it interpretive relevant that part of our stock of knowledge at hand
> has "something to do" with the thematic object now given to our interpreta-
> tion; but,* uno actu, *certain particular moments of the object perceived obtain
> the character of major or minor relevance for the task of recognizing and
> interpreting the actually experienced segment of the world.* (Schutz 2011, 113;
> Schutz's emphasis)

As I said, also interpretive relevances are either intrinsic or imposed.

> The first guess, originating in the passive synthesis of recognition, certainly
> lacks any volitional character. Automatically, so to speak (that is, by means of
> passive synthesis), the object is perceived as being "similar," "like," "of the
> type as," this and that typically already experienced object. (Schutz 2011, 116)

It is not merely perceived as "something" indefinite but, from the outset,
as something definite. As soon as I am aware, my first interpretation is moot
because the interpretative relevances which founded my first guess "are not
unequivocally determinable—they may hold good for another interpretation
which is incompatible with the first one" (Schutz 2011, 117).

Motivational relevances, finally, refer to two different kinds of situations
according to the motives involved. The concept of motive might refer, in
some cases, "to the idea of the state of affairs to be brought about by the
action which impels us to act" (Schutz 2011, 120), which "is phantasized by
us before we start our action. We call this kind of motive the 'in-order-to'
motive of our acting" (Schutz 2011, 120).

> If I place myself at the moment *before* I begin to act, merely projecting the
> state of affairs to be brought about and the single steps relevant for actualizing
> this goal, I may say that the phantasied state of affairs aimed at motivates the

single steps to be taken for its actualization. If, however I place myself at a moment *after my action has already begun,* I may express exactly the same situation by means of a chain of "because" sentences. (Schutz 2011, 120–121; Schutz's emphasis)

As a consequence, there are two kinds of motivational relevances: the "in-order-to" type and the "because" type. In-order-to motives are arranged, and they can even be integrated with one another into a plan. However, they are "founded on a set of genuine because motives sedimented in the biographically determined situation of the self at a particular moment" (Schutz 2011, 130).

As we know, motivational relevances can either be intrinsic or imposed. Schutz is "especially interested in the socially imposed motivational relevances" (Schutz 2011, 122) because, once the paramount project is constituted, all motivational relevances deriving from it "are experienced as being imposed" (Schutz 2011, 123). Furthermore, all relevance systems are socially determined (Schutz and Luckmann 1989, 290). This means that, as relevances are originated "in the passive synthesis of recognition," they lack any "volitional character.

SOCIALIZATION AND THE
SOCIOLOGY OF KNOWLEDGE

Schutz describes social determination as an imposition of the social world upon the individual, who finds himself always in the midst of a social environment which is a "co-constitutive" element of his biographical situation and is therefore "experienced as inescapably belonging to it" (Schutz and Luckmann 1989, 278). It is a determination—not just any element—of his situation because it determines every "interest and the relevance systems of all sorts—motivational, thematic, interpretative" (Schutz and Luckmann 1989, 278).

Social determination, if held over time, produces socialization. Schutz develops his own perspective on this matter, in terms of a "*socialization of the type-formation of human action*" which includes typifications of the Other, self-typifications and "types of courses-of-action, motive, and personality" (Schutz and Luckmann 1989, 212). It is a "whole system of types under which any social group experiences itself [which] has to be learned by a process of acculturation" (Schutz and Luckmann 1989, 290).

A significant aspect of socialization is the learning of the various markings and indications "for the position, status, role, and prestige each individual occupies or has within the stratification of the group" (Schutz and Luckmann

1989, 290). In order to find its bearings in the group, the individual has to know the different ways of behaving and has to learn to distinguish "the manifold badges, insignias, and emblems which are approved by the group as indicating social status and therefore as socially relevant" (Schutz and Luckmann 1989, 290). They show what typical behavior, actions and motives one may expect from others according to their position, status, role, and prestige.

> In a word, I have to learn the typical social roles and the typical expectations of behavior of the incumbents of such roles, in order myself to assume an appropriate corresponding role and display appropriate corresponding behavior expected to be approved by the social group. At the same time, I have to learn the typical distribution of knowledge prevailing in this group, and this involves knowledge of the appresentational, interpretative and [other] referential schemes that each of the subgroups takes for granted and applies to the respective appresentational indications. (Schutz and Luckmann 1989, 290)

So far, I have quoted Schutz speaking of status, role, prestige, and the like. He sounds like a mainstream sociologist of his days. . . . Is there anything phenomenological in his reflections on socialization? Yes, there is because Schutz situates these types in the relative natural worldview. There, they are "located ahead of the social group" which holds this worldview as: (a) "a component of socially approved type-formation"; (b) "a store of socio-culturally derived knowledge that is usually communicated traditionally"; (c) "standardized forms of the stock of knowledge with predesignated relevance structures whose conformity is warranted by genetic socialization"; (d) and "type-formations" which can even "lead to institutionalization" (Schutz and Luckmann 1989, 212).

As just seen, socialization is defined by Schutz as the learning of a stock of knowledge socially approved and derived. So, the sociology of socialization is intrinsically related to the sociology of knowledge. Once again, Schutz outlines his own perspective on this matter.

In the manuscripts preparatory for his last book, *Structures of the Life-World*, Schutz focuses on two of the main problems of the sociology of knowledge: the social structure and the social derivation of the stock of knowledge. He claims that the stock of knowledge is socially structured since "only a small fraction of the stock of knowledge at hand [is] originated from the individual's own experience," while "the greater portion is socially derived and has been handed down to him by parents and teachers as so-called social heritage" (Schutz and Luckmann 1989, 288).

Social heritage "consists of a set of systems of relevant typifications, of typical solutions for typical practical and theoretical problems, of typical precepts for typical behavior, including the pertinent systems of appresentational references" (Schutz and Luckmann 1989, 288). In other words, socially approved knowledge consists "in a set of recipes designed to help each member of the group to define and determine his situation in the reality of everyday life in a typical way" (Schutz and Luckmann 1989, 288). Thus, socially derived knowledge must include typifications "of social relations, of social forms of intercommunication, of social stratification taken for granted by the group, and therefore socially approved by it" (Schutz and Luckmann 1989, 290).

SYSTEMS OF RELEVANCES AND TYPIFICATIONS: A SYNTHESIS OF THE CORE CONCEPTS IN PHENOMENOLOGICAL SOCIOLOGY

So far, I have depicted phenomenological sociology as a group-oriented science dealing with issues such as socialization and social constraint, whose core concept is the concept of relevance.[10] As a final consideration, it might be useful to go through one of the papers that Schutz considered "applied theory" as an example of how all these issues can be integrated. In addition, it will help fighting another preconception about Schutz's phenomenological sociology: that it fails "to consider the community as a system that perpetuates itself through space and time" (Overgaard and Zahavi 2009, 111). To that aim, I will quote from one of the most important sociological papers of the late Schutz, "Equality and the meaning structure of the social world."

According to Schutz, man is born into a social world which "is experienced by him as a tight knot web of social relationships, [. . .] of institutionalized forms of social organization, of systems of status and prestige, etc." that are taken for granted "for those living within it" (Schutz 1964, 230). In William Graham Sumner's terminology, "the folkways of the in-group, which are socially accepted as the good ways and the right ways for coming to terms with things and fellow-men [. . .] are taken for granted because they have stood the test so far, and, being socially approved, are held as requiring neither an explanation nor a justification" (Schutz 1964, 230–231).

Folkways "constitute the social heritage which is handed down to children born into and growing up within the group," also "the approaching stranger who wants to be accepted by the group" has to learn by acculturation (Schutz 1964, 231). It not only establishes "the standard in terms of which the in-group 'defines its situation'"; it also becomes an element of the actual situation since it originates in previous situations defined by the group (Schutz 1964, 231).

The network of typifications we are referring to includes what Talcott Parsons called system, role, status, role expectation, and the like. They are "typifications of human individuals, of their course-of-action patterns, of their motives and goals, or of the sociocultural products which originated in their actions" and which were formed in the main by others—our predecessors and contemporaries—as "tools for coming to terms with things" accepted by the group as social derived knowledge (Schutz 1964, 235).

Socially approved typifications are "organized in domains of relevances which form, in turn, a system and are elements of what Scheler called the relative natural conception of the world" (Schutz 1964, 228). A system of relevances and typifications "functions as both a scheme of interpretation and as a scheme of orientation for each member of the in-group and constitutes therewith a universe of discourse among them" (Schutz 1964, 237). Members share a subjective meaning of the group, which

> consists in their knowledge of a common situation, and with it of a common system of typifications and relevances. This situation has its history in which the individual members' biographies participate; and the system of typification and relevances determining the situation forms a common relative natural conception of the world. Here the individual members are "at home." That is, they find their bearings without difficulty in the common surroundings, guided by a set of recipes of more or less institutionalized habits, mores, folkways, etc., that help them come to terms with beings and fellow-men belonging to the same situation. The system of typifications and relevances shared with the other members of the group defines the social roles, positions, and statutes of each. (Schutz 1964, 251–252)

Group memberships not only have a subjective but also an objective meaning. That is why we should take into account not just "the point of view of those who consider themselves members of it and speak of one another in terms of 'We'" (Schutz 1964, 254), but also "the point of view of outsiders who speak of its members in terms of 'They'" (Schutz 1964, 255). In this regard, "the notion of the group is a conceptual construct of the outsider. By the operation of *his* system of typifications and relevances he subsumes individuals showing certain particular characteristics and traits under a social category that is homogenenous merely from his, the ousider's, point of view" (Schutz 1964, 255; Schutz's emphasis). His interpretation of the group "will never fully coincide with the self-interpretation by the in-group" (Schutz 1964, 255). This discrepancy

> remains relatively harmless, so long as the individuals thus typified are not subject to the outsider's control. [. . .] If, however, the outsider has the power to impose his system of relevances upon the individuals typified by him, and especially to enforce its institutionalization, then this fact will create various

repercussions on the situation of the individuals typified against their will. (Schutz 1964, 255)

Three major issues for phenomenological sociology are mentioned here: (a) the problem of relevances (with a particular accent on its systemic properties and on power relations); (b) institutions conceived as social forces; (c) and social constraint. These issues are, in turn, related one to each other. Relevances are "accepted beyond question by the particular sociocultural environment" (Schutz 1964, 253). They are lived by the members of an in-group as sanctioned knowledge and experienced in terms of institutionalized patterns to be interiorized (Schutz 1964, 253). However, "the members of an out-group do not hold the ways of life of the in-group as self-evident truth" (Schutz 1964, 245). On the contrary, they measure "the standards prevailing in the group under consideration in accordance with the system of relevances prevailing within the natural aspect the world has [. . . for their] homegroup" (Schutz 1964, 246). This gives raise to "the various means of social control," which serve the purpose of standardizing and institutionalizing the schemes of typifications (Schutz 1964, 238). As I already said, institutions not only have a subjective dimension (as interiorized cultural patterns) but also an objective dimension. Schutz mentions as an example "administrative and legislative measures" that places "individuals under imposed social categories" such as tax laws, income classes, draft laws, rent laws, and so forth (Schutz 1964, 255–256). For being imposed, this kind of relevances and typifications "will hardly achieve the effect that those subjected to it consider themselves members of a We-group" (Schutz 1964, 256). They are meant to be "imposed group membership and imposed systems of relevances" (Schutz 1964, 228).

The conclusion follows that phenomenological sociology does not disregard the systemic properties of the social but offers an alternative approach. Social roles, status, and the like are addressed as social typifications which are, to some extent, imposed relevances with which members have to come to terms. Impositions, in turn, are not enforced by "the System" over the individuals but by groups one over the others. If maintained over time, imposed relevances can become institutionalized and serve as means of social control.

NOTES

1. I present an extended version of my argument in favor of Embree's stance on the first person plural perspective and collective subjects, in a paper published in *Schutzian Research* 9 (Belvedere 2017).

2. It is not only that Schutz's sociology does not take the individual as a starting point. He also considered that most social relations are abstract and relatively

impersonal: "Only in the we-relationship of the surrounding world do the partners, by their mutual biographical involvement, experience one another as unique individuals. In all the other dimensions of the social world—that of contemporaries, predecessors, and successors—a fellowman is not experienced in his individual uniqueness but in a series of typifications—typical behavior-patterns" (Schutz and Luckmann 1989, 291). Accordingly—while discussing the "grounding of the concepts" of social role, social stratification, institutional behavior, organizational behavior, sociology of professions, prestige and social status, etc.—Schutz claims that, by means of typifications, "the other person is always grasped only in partial contents and partial functions of his self, never in his uniqueness in a unique concrete situation. He seems to be given to the observer or partner only with a part of his self; with one part he always remains outside the social relationship" (Schutz and Luckmann 1989, 212).

3. In other papers, Schutz was critical of Durkhiem's idea of a collective consciousness (Schutz 1966, 38–39; 1967, 144); latter, he came to realize that there is some phenomenology in Durkheim. Counter to ideas he expressed elsewhere, in "Problems of a Sociology of Language," Schutz showed some agreement with Durkheim. Also, he had in mind to develop further his personal reading of Durkheim, as can be seen in his notebooks about the structures of the life-world, where he writes: "Here perhaps a digression on: Durkheim: collective consciousness" (Schutz and Luckmann 1989, 212; see also Schutz and Luckmann 1989, 265).

4. In this perspective, Durkheim's work can be seen as phenomenological. Indeed, that is my claim in "Durkheim as the founding father of phenomenological sociology" (Belvedere 2015a). However, here I will strictly focus on the concept of collective consciousness.

5. Also Paoletti (2002, 438, 444) agrees with this.

6. According to Husserl, the word "intentionality" refers to "this universal fundamental property of consciousness: to be consciousness *of* something; as a *cogito,* to bear within itself its *cogitatum*" (Husserl 1982, 33). Inasmuch Durkheim is dealing with the correlation of the subjective and the objective—for instance, with the distinction of individual and collective representations (Durkheim 2004b)—it can be said that he takes intentionality for granted.

7. Schutz's reflections on the problem of relevance are among the most important contributions he ever made to phenomenological sociology. However, they also have philosophical implications of great import. I address these consequences in a recent paper (Belvedere 2021).

8. Arvidson (2018, 28ff.) also finds this relation between relevance and intentionality in his comments on Gurwitsch's theory of the marginal halo.

9. Other classical concepts of Husserlian phenomenology are putt together in Schutz's theory of relevance, such as the attentional ray of consciousness, the theory of constitution, inner and outer horizons, the phenomenological time, and the like.

10. Göttlich (2014, 90) as well considers that the problem of relevance is one of the main "thematic fields" in sociology. See also Muzzetto (2006, part 2).

Chapter Three

The Specific Method of Phenomenological Sociology

Any discipline must have a method that suits its object. If phenomenology—including its sociological uses—starts and ends with "things themselves," then it is the object that determines the method, since the path leading to them must adequate the things addressed. In other words, the method must fit its object.

As has been argued in chapter 2, the distinctive object of phenomenological sociology is the natural attitude of groups. This imposes specific conditions to its method. On the one hand, it must be phenomenological—conceiving phenomenology, in line with our previous claims, as a description of the natural attitude according to the Schutzian tradition. On the other hand, it must be sociological. This is exactly the subject to be addressed in this chapter.

In the following, I will argue that the main methodological resources of phenomenological sociology are the *epoché*, the eidetic reduction, and the constitutional analysis of the natural attitude as applied to the study of group phenomena; that is, not as used in the perspective of the first person singular but in that of the first person plural—even if we can also deal with the second and the third persons, since, as far as the sociological perspective is involved, they are always addressed from the group's standpoint. Even more, it is a central claim of phenomenological sociology that (as seen in chapter 2) the first person perspective is informed by the group's natural relative worldview. In accordance, I will illustrate how these resources are applied to the study of groups by making some theoretical claims and giving examples of how classical and contemporary thinkers have practiced them.

THE *EPOCHÉ* OF THE NATURAL
ATTITUDE OF GROUPS

As seen in chapter 1, while the philosophical *epoché* suspends our belief in the reality of the world by placing it within brackets, in our natural attitude we exercise a different kind of *epoché* by which we suspend doubt in its existence. What we put into brackets is the doubt that the world and its objects might be otherwise than they appear to us (Schutz 1996, 27; see also Schutz 1962, 229–230, Schutz 1996, 110–111). This is what the very term "natural attitude" means: that we simply accept "as real phenomena presented to it without asking whether or not they are truly being or illusion, as long as its experiencings of these phenomena are consistent" and remain consistent (Schutz 2013, 281).

However, this attitude of taking the world as it is does not involve any predicative positing. In this regard, Morley makes a significant distinction:

> The mundane *epoché* is an unfocused unreflective *epoché* that constrains experience and drives our awareness within the limitations of the natural attitude. In contrast, the phenomenological *epoché* is a focused, self-reflective, and disciplined *epoché* that offers options and possibilities for our understanding of the world in a manner best described as liberating. (Morley 2010, 229–230)

In addition, we do not acquire the natural attitude by an act of judging (Schutz 1996, 111) but by means of pragmatic motives (Schutz 1996, 27) because "we have not a theoretical but an eminently practical interest" in this world, which it is for us not an object of thought but a field of dominations. As seen in chapter 1, as long as the established schemes of reference work and "the actions and operations performed under its guidance yield the desired results, in the natural attitude we are not interested whether this world does 'really' exist or whether it is only a coherent system of consistent appearances" (Schutz 1996, 26). As Barber (2017, 3) notes, the world of everyday life "is a distinctive domain in which we live prior to any theorizing about it."

There are at least two possible ways to deal with the natural attitude of groups; one descriptive, another experimental. However, both involve the intent to grasp group's phenomena accessing them, methodologically, from the insider's point of view; taking this term in the sense it has for Embree (2015, 95), which not only connotates individual meaning but also (and this is what interests us here) communal or collective meaning. In this view, the phenomenological sociologist deals with collective meaning, which he accesses through his own experience as an insider of a given group.

Consequently, the phenomenological sociologist does not deal with the phenomenological *epoché* practiced by the philosopher (seen in chapter 1) but with the natural *epoché* already performed by the members of a given group. In other words, he does not perform this *epoché* on his own but rather finds it already performed and imposed on him as a group member—that is, as an insider—through the system of relevances characteristic to the group he belongs to.

As far as we are a part of the group being studied, that view is ours but not merely as a personal experience: it is that aspect of our consciousness socially shaped by the imposed relevances mentioned in chapter 2. As group's members we all accept as self-evident the ideas, beliefs, habits, and so forth, considered a part of the natural way of life of those who are "one of us." So, the natural attitude with which the phenomenological sociologist deals is a group attitude, even though he can access it from his personal point of view. To do that, we have to focus on the relevances imposed on us, not on our personal intrinsic relevances. Only by doing that we can access the social in us.

Now, we said many times that, in the *epoché* of the natural attitude, we take for granted things as they are. How can we deal with this naïve and dogmatic kind of assumptions since we are supposed not to notice that which we take for granted? There are two ways to do this: one, descriptive; another, experimental. Either spontaneously we naturally note, in our everyday life, that things do not work as expected; or deliberately we modify our natural expectations to notice that which we have taken for granted so far. Let us now see how to deal practically with this methodological resource. I will illustrate the use of the *epoché* of groups with examples taken from the works of Michel Barber and Harold Garfinkel.

As seen in the previous chapters, the natural attitude suspends the doubt that things might be otherwise until further notice. It means that the natural attitude can be challenged and that it is not meant to last forever but only until a counter proof comes out. This can happen "naturally," in the course of events we spontaneously live in our everyday life. There are many reasons why things can turn out to be different than we expected. Frustrated expectations, social changes, social crisis, social conflicts are some among numerous possible causes of a breakdown of the natural attitude of groups. Also unexpected events, surprises, and a good dose of serendipity may help us perceive certain aspects of our natural attitude.

A nice instantiation of this kind of descriptive approach to the *epoché* of the natural attitude of groups is Barber's study on the *epoché* of humor. His claim is that "the comic *epoché* removes one from the pressures of working, standing outside the assumptions and habits of everyday life and abstracting from them" (Barber 2017, 183). However, it does "not only facilitate disengagement"; it also "turn us more attentively to experience" (Barber 2017, 183). This is how it works.

As such, the entrance into an encompassing comic attitude through the *epoché* actually involves a comprehensive stance, an all-embracing *intentional* posture, a large-scale *aiming* at reality in relation to which all reality will be given, similar to but more comprehensive than smaller intentional acts like those of memory, perception, willing, or valuing. Within this encompassing intentional framework, one experiences the thwarting of the lower-level intentional acts that are found within the framework and that provide pleasure.

Moreover, as happens within the phenomenological *epoché*, one is at a remove from one's everyday experiences and beliefs, and correlatively the intentional actions and statements made within this province are no longer seen as they would be in everyday life. Seen within the humorous attitude, statements that would be insulting or rude in everyday life, for instance, become comical and take on a humorous significance. It is as though they undergo a kind of transvaluation—grasped in an entirely different light. (Barber 2017, 152–153)

Also, the *epoché* pries the interlocutors

loose from the rigidly defined roles of pragmatic everyday life. The new form of spontaneity they take up together aims at producing humor together instead of harvesting a cotton field and garnering profits. A relaxed tension of conscious permits the release of bottled up feelings of aggression and anger, softened by humor. The interlocutors experience themselves differently from how they experience themselves in everyday life, however much they may still have one foot in that world. (Barber 2021, 168)

Well, how do we get to know about this kind of *epoché*? How is the descriptive approach to the group's *epoché* to proceed?

According to Barber, "one sign that the comic *epoché* transports partners into a self-enclosed province of meaning is that [. . .] partners in humor need to alert each other to the fact that they are *exiting* the province, by signaling through an utterance such as 'And now, seriously . . .' or by flashing some bodily signal" (Barber 2017, 182). Also, one may begin

with a formulaic statement (e.g., "Did you hear the joke about . . . "); or with a smile or wink indicating that one is entering with another the territory of humor in which everyday rules no longer hold and narratives (such as in jokes) ought not to be taken as factually true; or with a comment that seems so comically outrageous that one recognizes immediately that a new sphere of meaning has supervened. (Barber 2021, 154)

Interesting to note are our consociates in the interaction of everyday life who invite us to leap into the finite province of humor by performing this *epoché*. We may say that it works as an "instructed action" in Garfinkel's (2002, 219–218) sense. We learn to perform this *epoché* not on our own but following instructions given by someone else, who—as Barber (2017, 151) beautifully says—invites us "to leap together" into a different province of meaning.

Barber offers a few examples of how this happens in everyday life. See, for instance, his account of the comic *epoché* in an occasion he shared with "a long-time African-American friend" whose humor he had come "to appreciate over many years" (Barber 2017, 153). This is his story:

> Once, he was walking through a store with me, and he greeted three white persons, none of whom returned a response. After the third non-response, he turned to me and said, "I have just greeted three white persons and none of them responded to me; what is wrong with you people?" We both burst out laughing. (Barber 2017, 153)

I would like to highlight a number of wonderful findings here. First, it is an intersubjective *epoché* that is not performed by the solitary ego but by two friends, one of which invites the other to bracket some features of the natural attitude in which they both lived so far, in order to see them from a different angle and to call into question the assumptions accepted as members of the group—let's say, as members of a democratic society, where people are supposed to be polite.

Second, it is not an originary *epoché* since it works upon a previous one, the *epoché* of the natural attitude. In this sense, all *epochai* are secondary except that of the natural attitude. Even the phenomenological *epoché* is so, since it starts with the natural attitude which—according to Schutz—is structured on an *epoché* of doubt. In the case of humor, that the *epoché* has already been performed when we get immersed in the situation is made evident by the fact that "societies throughout history have fenced off and isolated spatio-temporal sites that facilitate the comic *epoché*" (Barber 2017, 182).[1] In other words, *epochai* like the comic *epoché* are often institutionalized.

Third, both friends were socialized as members of the same group; however, they have different perspectives on it. That is why one of them is aware of the situation that, even thou they are supposed to be a part of the same group—which is, obviously, the white perspective—they really belong to different groups (which he expresses by referring to "you people"). This friend had already questioned practically the predominant view of the group as inclusive and equalitarian. It is not the reflective attitude but practical troubles in everyday life that lead him to suspend those assumptions.

Fourth, what calls into question the group's natural attitude is not a new idea, a fresh perspective, nor anything alike. It is pure and simply social conflict—specifically in this case, racism.[2] Once denaturalized racists prejudices and practices, it becomes evident that what we have is not one integrated group (as the dominant group wants to see it) but two groups in conflict.

Finally, true politeness comes from this friend who, with a joke, kindly makes evident for both friends that they can get along once disconnected from those prejudices, which allows them to integrate a different kind of group. So, the outcome of this practical *epoché* is not just a new perspective but a new configuration of the group and of group relationships.

However, it may happen that we want to conduct a research on a group we do not belong to. How can we deal with this kind of situation? The first thing to do is—as the ethnomethodologists say—become a member of the social setting we are to address. To that end, we must get "vulgarly competent" at what members do, which means to acquire "unique adequacy."

Members use their methods to make phenomena observable and to provide for descriptions of ordinary things (Garfinkel 2002, 101). In this view, to be a member is to recognize what is evident for everyone, to know what everyone knows, and to be capable of "doing" what everybody does. So, to be a member is to have a kind of mastery—for instance, the "mastery of natural language" (see Garfinkel and Sacks 1986, 160, and Heritage 1992, 155).

In this respect, members are "skillful" (Garfkinkel and Sacks 1986, 170), which means that they are "unanimous" in some respects, that their methods are "unavoidably used" in a certain way, and that their practices are somewhat invariant (Garfinkel and Sacks 1986, 173). All this leads to the idea that members can make an "adequate application" of precepts based on their competence (Garfinkel and Sacks 1986, 176) and produce an orderly social setting. It also requires that one has "to become 'vulgarly competent' with the methods" studied. Not only would one "have to learn by doing," but one's "mastery itself would provide the basis for, and subject of," our investigations (Lynch 1999, 218).

It follows from Lynch's descriptions that, once we become vulgarly competent, we can take our doing as an object of research. However, it is not our personal, idiosyncratic doing. Once we have become a member of a social setting, and as long as we focus on our doing as what any competent member would do, we can address that group's natural attitude. Yet, we would still be practicing a descriptive phenomenology of the group's natural attitude, in line with the example taken from Barber. However, we can go one step further and experiment with that attitude. This will allow us to access the intersubjective work of producing a local order.

It was Garfinkel who found the most radical way to address the natural attitude of groups. According to Psathas (2004, 22), the breaching experiments he ideated work, to some extent, as a practical *epoché* since they serve to alter the normally perceived to motivate member's work for producing an order. They involve a bracketing of the presuppositions and theories about the social world.

Garfinkel wondered how a person would look at "an ordinary and famil-iar scene and what will he see in it if we require of him that he do no more than look at it as something that for him it 'obviously' and 'really' is not" (Garfinkel 1994, 44). With that aim he asked his students to view themselves at home as if they were boarders in the household (Garfinkel 1994, 45). He found out that for many of them it was a difficult attitude to maintain "because with it quarreling, bickering, and hostile motivations became discomfitingly visible" (Garfinkel 1994, 46). Then he asked his students to not just imagine they were a boarder, but also to act like one: "They were instructed to con-duct themselves in a circumspect and polite fashion" (Garfinkel 1994, 47). Most family members were "stupefied" and "vigorously sought to make the strange actions intelligible and to restore the situation to normal appearances" (Garfinkel 1994, 45). They also "demanded explanations."

As can be appreciated, Garfinkel ideated what we may call "a practical *epoché*." He did not ask his students just to adopt a reflective attitude. He sent them into the life-world to interact with others, to practice the bracketing of our natural assumptions in the midst of things themselves. And—as we can see—it is much harder, and it has way more consequences, to act as a stranger than just to view oneself as one.

EIDETIC ANALYSIS IN PHENOMENOLOGICAL SOCIOLOGY

Once described the natural attitude of groups, we can perform its eidetic analysis. In phenomenology, eidetic reduction "involves an effort at free variation, at considering the various mediations of phenomena to determine 'essential' features of those phenomena" (Gordon 1995, 15). However, this search for the essence is not "essentialistic"; on the contrary, it points out "the errors of collapsing beings into 'substances' ('necessary beings')" (Gordon 2000, 155–156). Gordon (2008, 124) calls this "a form of constructivist view of essence" because it is a view that "does not eliminate contingency from the world" (Gordon 2008, 124).

In chapter 1, we have seen how the eidetic reduction is performed on the already phenomenologically reduced sphere. Nevertheless—as Morley (2010, 226) penetratingly notes—"the eidetic reduction is contingent on the domain or discipline within which one is working as well as the particular phenomenon being studied." By performing it, we can "suspend existential assumptions about a particular phenomenon, or [. . .] view it only within a particular frame of interest or disciplinary domain" (Morley 2010, 226). Thus, the issue at stake is not eidetic analysis at large (as seen in chapter 1) but the peculiar way in which it is conducted in phenomenological sociology.

Phenomenological sociology is an eidetic mundane science dealing with invariant, peculiar, and essential structures of the mind—in particular, of a society composed of living minds. As Barber notes, Schutz

> deploys an eidetic methodology to determine the essential features of everyday life [. . .] Such essential structures of the social world would include such facts as that we always employ typification—and relevance—systems in everyday life, that we always deal with objective and subjective meanings in interpreting each other, and that we always relate to each as face-to-face Consociates or as Contemporaries, Predecessors, and Successors. (Barber 2017, 4)

A similar conception is found in Durkheim and Garfinkel. Regarding the godfather of academic sociology, once performed the *epoché*, he engages in eidetic reduction inquiring, in chapter 1 of *Rules of Sociological Method*, "What is a social fact?"[3] After bracketing our preconceptions, we can "see the apparently most arbitrary facts to then display, to a more thorough observation, features of regularity and persistence that constitute the symptoms of its objectivity" (Durkheim 1999, 28).

Another aspect of the "intrinsic feature of these facts" is that "they are endowed with a constraining and imperative power, by means of which they are imposed" upon the individual (Durkheim 1999, 4) so that they "consist in manners of acting, thinking, feeling, external to the individual, endowed with a certain power of constraint" (Durkheim 1999, 5). Briefly, the eidetic structure of social facts consists in ways of acting that are "capable of exerting over the individual an external constraint" (Durkheim 1999, 14).

What Durkheim called "constraint" is not so different from what Buttler (1990, 273) calls "punitive consequences." In this view, essences are not only (neither mainly) constituted in free arbitrariness by the individual but, on the contrary, socially inflicted—in line with what has been seen in chapter 2 when showed that, according to Schutz, the main sociological concept is that of "imposed relevances." Consequently, what makes up and keeps unchanged the invariant features of the social is that "collective consciousness at work" that Schutz mentioned in his latest years.

Accordingly, the phenomenological approach "requires an expansion of the conventional view" (Buttler 1990, 272). Regarding our question, the most important aspect to be attended to is the "clearly punitive consequences" of social acts and performances. For instance, "those who fail to do their gender right are regularly punished" (Buttler 1990, 273). In this light, gender is

> a construction that regularly conceals its genesis. The tacit collective agreement to perform, produce, and sustain discrete and polar genders as cultural fictions is obscured by the credibility of its own production. The authors of gender become entranced by their own fictions whereby the construction compels one's belief

in its necessity and naturalness. The historical possibilities materialized through various corporeal styles are nothing other than those punitively regulated cultural fictions that are alternately embodied and disguised under duress. (Buttler 1990, 273)

Those constancies once established, can be explored sociologically. This has been accomplished in the most novel way by Garfinkel, who performed *more suo* the eidetic reduction. For instance, in an experiment in which he used "inverting lenses" (Garfinkel 2002, 207ff.) to "*become strange again* with the ways of practical action as worldly stuff" (Garfinkel 2002, 210, Garfinkel's emphasis), he determined that, in the "phenomenal details" of the "*in vivo* stream of practices," there is "an invariant," "a structure," such as, that "there are constancies" (Garfinkel 2002, 209).

This is a peculiar way to conduct eidetic analysis, since Garfinkel does not deal with pure consciousness but with "worldly stuff." The constancies referred to are situational. Garfinkel certainly focused on members' work to assign meaning and produce a social order, but that kind of work is not merely personal: it is a collective accomplishment.

Garfinkel considered these constancies in accordance with Gurwitsch's conception of *Gestalt*,

> which, although much modified, became important in Garfinkel's later work, particularly in his focus on the phenomenal field properties of social things. Through Gurwitsch, Garfinkel came to understand that the witnessable and recognizable properties of social phenomena come together in the *gestalt* coherence of what he came to call the phenomenal field properties of oriented objects. (Warfield Rawls 2002, 14)

It must be stressed that Garfinkel "deliberately" misread "Gurwitsch's theory of the coherence of objects[4] as to provide for the concertedly achieved coherence of sociology's organizational things" (Garfinkel 2002, 167). By doing this, he managed "to appropriate to the interests of EM investigations and its policies and methods, the topics and themes of *gestalt* phenomena" and rename them as "a figuration of details" (Garfinkel 2002, 167). Thus, what Garfinkel did was not just a reading but rather a creative appropriation from "phenomenological studies" (Garfinkel 2002, 176).

Garfinkel (2002, 176) found particularly interesting Gurwitsch's "transcendental phenomenological examination and respecification of the *Gestalt* theory of form" because it "provided for the achieved coherence of objects with the properties of functional significance" (Garfinkel 2002, 176). He also reported "*as a finding* the endogenous relevance to a developing contexture of recognizable constituent significations entirely from within the stream of perception. (Garfinkel 2002, 176; Garfinkel's emphasis).

It was also Gurwitsch who inspired Garfinkel's idea that members' methods "endogenously" exhibit "standing topical relevance to the local order producing parties of descriptive adequacy and evidence [. . .] 'Only endogenously' is elaborated with reference to Gurwitsch's respecified generics of *gestalt* theory and principles" (Garfinkel 2002, 73), which now must become empirically specified in actual cases. Since topics of order are "thick" in and with "phenomenal details" (Garfinkel 2002, 166), they can be described in terms of "Gurwitsch's transcendental phenomenological description of the functional significations and their relations of contexture" (Garfinkel 2002, 166, n. 25).

Another idea that Garfinkel borrowed from Gurwitsch is the notion of "salience."

> The constituent, "Salience," is explained by Ethnomethodology's having appropriated to the problem of social order in the social sciences Gurwithsch's magisterial result in *Field of Consciousness:* Salience abbreviates the endogenous coherence of a figure of organized gestalt contexture that emerges upon its background, disengaged from its background. (Garfinkel 2002, 281)

Briefly, the notions of Gestalt, endogenous relevance, and salience were respecified by Garfinkel in a way that allow to better appreciate the intrinsic configuration of group phenomena. With this he made unmatched contributions to eidetic analysis in phenomenological sociology.

CONSTITUTIONAL ANALYSIS OF THE
NATURAL ATTITUDE OF GROUPS

As seen in chapter 1, Schutz conceived of constitutive phenomenology of the natural attitude as phenomenological psychology, which is a "psychological apperception of the natural attitude" (Schutz 1962, 132). Within this framework, the phenomenological psychologist must "remain 'on the ground of inner appearance as the appearance of that which is peculiar to the psychic'" (Schutz 1967, 44). Therefore, phenomenological psychology does not deal with "matters of fact" but must "become aprioristic" and "deal with the 'Eidos,' with the essence of thoughts" (Schutz 1966, 6).

In this view, the phenomenological method would contribute "to the establishment of the cultural sciences[5] [. . .] bringing to light a style of thought peculiar to these sciences by an analysis of the constitutive activities of the transcendental subjectivity" since all sciences dealing with "cultural phenomena [. . .] are related to that mundane sphere which transcendental phenomenology has bracketed" and nevertheless is accessible to "a psychology oriented to everyday life" (Schutz 1962, 122) aiming at "showing the intentional accomplishments of the transcendental subjectivity" by means of a constitutive phenomenology pursued as "a true science of mind (*Geist*)" and validated as "the only method [. . . for] a radical explanation of the world through mind" (Schutz 1962, 123).

Within this framework, the phenomenological social and cultural sciences do not deal with merely experienced but with eidetic objects which can only be accessed in full in the phenomenologically reduced sphere. This situation poses a problem for "all the hitherto existing cultural and social sciences" since they merely relate "to phenomena of mundane intersubjectivity. [. . .] Hence, the transcendental constitutive phenomena, which only become visible in the phenomenologically reduced sphere, scarcely come within" their view (Schutz 1967, 132). Only through the phenomenological reduction we can access the stream of consciousness "as a realm of its own in its absolutely unique nature" in order to "experience it and describe its inner structure" (Schutz 1966, 5–6).

Schutz considered it "highly unlikely" that the social scientist and the layperson would turn their attention to the various strata of meaning upon which their comprehension of their conduct is based and that necessarily must be attended to in order to explicate the structures of the social world that "are the foundation of the constructs" by which their "motives and actions are interpreted" (Schutz 1964, 21).

Obviously, phenomenological sociology cannot abide by this method, even if Schutz' phenomenological psychology perfectly suits the needs of other kinds of sciences. Phenomenological sociology, instead, deals with empirical phenomena. Sure, it has—as any other science—an eidetic level, but it necessitates an empirical approach since it must reach for the autochthonous coherence of the phenomenal details produced in vivo as a collective accomplishment. Thus, once addressed that eidetic level (as we have done in the previous section), it needs to proceed differently in order to reach the empirical aspect of its specific object. The most elaborated and original contribution to the search for procedures to grasp the empirical dimension of group phenomena is Garfinkel's experiments with the natural attitude of members.

Psathas's brilliantly argues that Garfinkel "engaged in a constitutive sociology of the natural attitude's relevance, use, and functioning, as well as the uncovering of the social and interactional resources used by members for its production and sustenance" (Psathas 2004, 19). To access these resources, we must bracket the presuppositions of the natural attitude. With that aim, Garfinkel developed a method called "ethnomethodological indifference" (Psathas 2012, 26), by which he neutralized all value assessing and gave professional and lay methods in sociology the same kind of attention. Then, he conceived "demonstration experiments" using the technique of "disturbing or introducing a 'nasty surprise' in interacting with others in order to demonstrate the presence of much that was taken for granted [. . .] by simply not performing those acts which they expected—or by performing acts which others did not have any 'reason' to expect" (Psathas 1968, 514). Bearing this technique in mind, "Garfinkel asked what would happen if the operative assumptions of the natural attitude could not be met in everyday situations? What would be revealed [. . .] about the ways in which the natural attitude itself was sustained?" (Psathas 2012, 28).

Garfkinkel's questions open the field of constitutional analysis of the natural attitude of groups. Breaching experiments work as a practical *epoché* since they bracket de facto the assumptions of the natural attitude of groups by experimental means. Also, this methodological technique allows the sociologist to witness the wealth of autochthonous methods and endogenous practices displayed by members to produce the local social order which they see as evident and take for granted. All the sociologist does is motivate and witness member's work and methods for producing a local order. Once again, we must follow Garfinkel's brilliant indications.

Exploring persons' reactions to "breaches of ordinary expectancies, to difficulties in sustaining aspects of the natural attitude," allows to uncover "the actual methods" used by members, to make the social structures of everyday activities achieve "their observable organization, sense, and accountability" (Psathas 2012, 28). To that aim, Garfinkel created a procedure consisting of modifying "the objective structure of a familiar, known-in-common environment by rendering the background expectancies inoperative," thus "subjecting a person to a breach of the background expectancies of everyday" (Garfinkel 1994, 54).

By doing so, Garfinkel turned Schutzian sociology into an empirical research program of the natural attitude. He found out, in his early years, that the natural attitude—which Schutz described mostly theoretically—can be explored empirically. This is one of the decisive findings of his PhD dissertation. Back then, Garfinkel was "beginning to consider the possibilities for [. . .] a sociology *of* the natural attitude rather than one that operated *within* the natural attitude" (Psathas 2009, 425; Psathas's emphasis).

With that aim, Garfinkel focused on Schutz's concept of "multiple realities" (Schutz 1967, 207–259). He operationalized the different features of the finite provinces of meaning so that they could become the object of experimental studies (Psathas 2009, 417–418). In chapters 7 to 13 of his dissertation, Garfinkel described the six structural features of every finite province of meaning as depicted by Schutz. Each chapter took its title from one of these features: "Form of Sociality"; "Mode of Givenness of the Self"; "Mode of Time Consciousness"; "The *Epoché*"; "Mode of Attention to Life"; "Form of Spontaneity"; "The Constructs of Cognitive Style in Their Relationship to

Each Other" (Psathas 2009, 412–413). As a whole, these features compose an intertwined ensemble with systemic properties. Garfinkel figures out that any failure in one of these features will have an overall effect. In particular, he discloses that the systemic character of the cognitive stile of any finite province of meaning would be disrupted if any failure or disappearance would be experimentally introduced. As a consequence, a disruption of the finite province of meaning would occur (Psathas 2009, 414).

For example, Gafkinkel inquired how a person—when confronted with changes in the way the Other is perceived, to the extent that the cognitive style of the finite province of meaning in which this occurs can no longer be held—"will attempt to re-interpret the situation, find congruencies if possible, revise" his assessment of his "own previously strongly held beliefs, etc" (Psathas 2009, 416–417). Within this framework, one of Garfinkel's interest was investigating "shifts in motivational accounts, protocol statements of disturbance, and devices for resolving the incongruity of having been in error about an obvious thing" (Psathas 2009, 417). In his research, Garfinkel proved that the natural attitude is a members' accomplishment.

These early findings are a precedent of what might be the most powerful and instructive procedures ever ideated by Garfinkel, the "breaching experiments." To some extent, they work as a practical *epoché* since they serve to alter the normally perceived, this time in order to motivate member's work for producing an order.

Already in his PhD dissertation, Garfinkel intended "to empirically study the ways in which disruptions of the assumptions made in the natural attitude are reacted to and made sense of by subjects in a situation demanding of choice" (Psathas 2009, 405). This perspective is taken to a new level in Garfinkel's masterwork, *Studies in Ethnomethodology*. There, he ideated a procedure consisting in modifying "the objective structure of a familiar, known-in-common environment by rendering the background expectancies inoperative," thus "subjecting a person to a breach of the background expectancies of everyday" (Garfinkel 1994, 54).

> Specifically, this modification would consist of subjecting a person to a breach of the background expectancies of everyday life while (a) making it difficult for the person to interpret his situation as a game, an experiment, a deception, a play, *i.e.*, as something other than the one known according to the attitude of everyday life as a matter of enforceable morality and action, (b) making it necessary that he reconstruct the "natural facts" but giving him insufficient time to manage the reconstruction with respect to required mastery of practical circumstances for which he must call upon his knowledge of the "natural facts," and (c) requiring that he manage the reconstruction of the natural facts by himself and without consensual validation. (Garfinkel 1994, 54)

Garfinkel expected the person would not have an alternative other than "to try to normalize the resultant incongruities within the order of events of everyday life" once the events had lost "their perceivedly normal character" and the member become "unable to recognize an event's status as typical," familiar, and meaningful (Garfinkel 1994, 54–55).

As an experimentation with the natural attitude, breaching experiments disclose deep rooted features of the natural attitude.[6] They reveal that, when experiencing such a huge commotion, members display multiple methodological resources to repair an order. Breaching experiments are meant to make observable member's cooperative work of restitution of an order.

However, breaching experiments are not the only means to deal with social constitutional processes. These can also be reached through a descriptive analysis of the background expectancies using qualitative methods. An outstanding instance of this kind of procedures is Waksler's description of how the Other was constituted in the social perception of the 1973 sniping at New Orleans.

The main question that leads her case study is: "What, then, is the Other made of? Out of what elements in any specific situation is an Other constituted?" (Waksler 2010, 75). Her account also provides a unique perspective on something which should get as much attention as constituting processes themselves but, to my surprise, has not yet been the object of further studies: the processes of unconstitution. It would be obvious—at least for those who deal sociologically with the natural attitude of groups—that most things which are constituted can also be unconstituted. However, no one else but Waksler seems to have noticed that.

In her case study, Waksler (2010, vii) describes "the ultimately unsuccessful search for a second sniper" that followed the killing of the first one. She offers the following claims as a framework of her analysis:

> Prior assumptions and expectations create a space for the Other. Immediate concerns and needs outline that space. The space thus created is filled in with common-sense ideas about what an Other is and is not capable of and with sights, sounds, and indications of turn-taking. These are linked by common-sense theories and speculation, all to some extent constrained by the outline. New or reformulated assumptions and evidence, however, can change the meaning of the constituent elements or change the very outline itself. When expectations change, when the existence of an Other is denied, the same evidence can, though with varying degrees of difficulty, be reinterpreted to support the nonexistence of that Other. In that process, both the evidence and those who provide it can come in for reassessment and reevaluation. (Waksler 2010, 9)

It follows from these claims, as well as from data analysis, that evidence is not static but itself socially constructed and, in accordance, has an "ambiguous nature" (Waksler 2010, 15). Regarding this case in particular:

> The evidence used to constitute an Other [. . .] was a pastiche of everyday life assumptions: the initial assumption that there simply was (or had to be) more than one sniper; assumptions about what one person is capable and incapable of doing; assumptions about the meaning of sights, sounds, and leavings (what was left behind); and speculation, including the postulation of a conspiracy, to blend the evidence into a coherent whole. (Waksler 2010, 16)

Some of these assumptions involved "ideas about physical possibilities. Persons are subject to physical laws, however those laws are formulated" (Waksler 2010, 17, 76). Also, persons are *subject to common-sense rules, notably here 'acting like a person'* [. . .] Common sense serves as a general framework for identifying an Other—an Other is someone who acts like an Other, and, if relevant, a specific kind of Other" (Waksler 2010, 77, Waksler's emphasis). On these grounds, it is to be determined "what one ordinary person is capable of doing," which also "leads to the issue of what one extraordinary person might accomplish" (Waksler 2010, 18).

Likewise, "others are taken to be seeable, capable of sound and thus hearable, and capable of movement and action" (Waksler 2010, 19). This does not only involve direct perceptions but also an important dose of interpretation, even speculations.

> Sights, sounds, and indications of action can thereby "stand for" an Other. Reciprocity, i.e., turn-taking, can serve as especially compelling evidence. Others can leave traces—objects and other tangible "artifacts." Speculation, including here conspiracy theories, can be used to fill in the emerging picture. The existence of a given Other may, nonetheless, remain relative and tentative. (Waksler 2010, 19)

Indeed, sounds are "ambiguous and require interpretive work" (Waksler 2010, 25). "Ricochets and echoes can confuse comprehension [. . .] . Voices too can be problematic, for inferences are required to determine who is speaking and to whom" (Waksler 2010, 25). All this requires an explanation, and "conspiracy theories and general speculation" may help by providing "ways to deal with the events as a meaningful whole" (Waksler 2010, 34). Accordingly, evidence needs to be legitimated. In this case study, it "was assessed and legitimated not only in terms of its content but also in relation to who offered it" (Waksler 2010, 37).

Notwithstanding, the constitution of an Other remains as merely plausible; plausibility being just "a starting point but not necessarily sufficient to confirm the existence of another" (Waksler 2010, 75–76). For instance,

> Signs of a kinetic/tactile-kinesthetic body may be reformulated to be signs of something else. Only in the absence of problems are such signs strongly evidentiary.
> Indications of present or past action can stand for the existence of an Other. Actions can stand for a person, but they may also be otherwise explained. Attributing actions to a specific actor involves inferences that, although plausible at the time, may be refuted retrospectively. (Waksler 2010, 76)

That is why "the assumption that there was more than one sniper, plausible as it was at first, [. . .] came to be seen as both troublesome and increasingly implausible. [. . .] Work proceeded to 'lose' the second sniper" (Waksler 2010, 41). While new evidence undermined the idea of a second sniper, earlier evidence—gathered when his existence "was assumed and supporting that assumption"—was reassessed and reassigned to unconstitute this Other: "The very features that were used to constitute the second sniper came to be used to unconstitute that sniper" (Waksler 2010, 44).

Unconstituting an Other is a move which "involves inferences drawn directly from old and new evidence (sightings, leavings, physical evidence) and the reworking of contradictory evidence. It also, and inevitably, entails new speculation to fill in the gaps" (Waksler 2010, 47). So reworked evidence served as a basis for unconstituting the second sniper by redistributing sights, sounds, and leavings, by reassessing "evidence of turn-taking," and by replacing old speculation for a new one (Waksler 2010, 49). Now the assumption that there was only one sniper "facilitated the reading of evidence to document that assumption" (Waksler 2010, 50).

Nevertheless, some witnesses "had difficulty with the conclusion that they had 'created' an Other" (Waksler 2010, 50). One may conjecture that this is so because the constitution of an Other does not take place in the individuals intimate experience but in social settings, which endows the constituted element with the force of social facts. Be this as it might, we can tell for sure that:

> Claims of an Other's existence may be either confirmed or denied by others present or by later analysts. The postulated reliability of those who claim (or deny) the existence of an Other becomes consequential, as do the conditions under which those claims were made—stress, limited visibility, confusing circumstances, danger. Claims may be presented along with social confirmation to forestall attributions of unreliability. [. . .] Social settings are thus relevant for the constitution of an Other as well as for sustaining or unconstituting

that Other, with important implications for the participants in those settings. (Waksler 2010, 77)

The conclusion follows that not always a "specific Other" is given in experience. This raises questions about givenness. In Waksler's view—which I borrow—the specific Other "can be constituted rather than directly grasped," which means that he is "'made' and may not stay 'made' or stay 'unmade.' The work of constitution or unconstitution continues" (Waksler 2010, 78).

A CASE STUDY (OR HOW THIS METHOD HELPED ME THROUGH IN A RESEARCH I CONDUCTED)

So far, examples have been given of how the different steps of the method in phenomenological sociology were used along the last two centuries. It still must be proved that it can work as one, integrated method. To that end, I will refer to one of my studies in the phenomenology of tango dancing. I do not intend to repeat what was already published but to explain, by making it explicit, how the different aspects of this method were involved in doing that research. The curious reader might better enjoy the paper published in *Schutzian Research* (Belvedere 2016), where I exposed in detail my findings. Here, instead, I will focus on the methodological aspects involved in the fieldwork, which were not made public so far. Then, the reader might think of this section as a kind of "backstage" of that research.

As seen so far, the method of phenomenological sociology starts with the description of an *epoché* already performed in groups. The phenomenological sociologist does not bracket anything on his own but rather discloses what everybody (him included) brackets as members of an in-group.

The study I conducted sprang from my passion for tango, which for long preexisted my sociological vocation. For five years I attended eighteen different *milongas*, not for the sake of scientific research but for my pleasure. During those years, I became a part of the *milonga*[7] scene. I was able to interact with numerous *milongueros* and to make sense of the social life going on there. I acquired the natural relative worldview of the typical *milonguero*. As a member of that large group of Tango enthusiasts, I took for granted what everybody does. I managed to make sense of ordinary things and was able to methodically construct other's talk to provide for the possible occurrence of their actions. My perception was structured in line with the natural attitude of those who lead the life of a tango fan.

As a *milonguero*—i.e., as a member of the group of people who leads the life of a *tanguero*—I was bracketing the following aspects of my natural world. I suspended the doubt about whether there is a better way of life. I felt a part of this community, by which I made an *epoché* of all diverging aspect of the local social life. In other words, I assumed that we were essentially all the same—that we felt alike, enjoyed the same kind of things; briefly, that all members of the *milonga* scene were unanimous. Honestly, I must say that I still hold in *epoché* all these features except one, which was practically questioned in an insightful way in a particular occasion.

One day, during my tango classes, the woman who was taking the lesson along with me, left her position as a student and started to unexpectedly assume a teaching role. Desperately she intended to teach me how to *marcar* (to indicate) by pressing her fingers into my back frenetically, trying to show me what to her was obvious but what to me was a mystery.

In the dance of tango, *"marcar"* (to indicate) and *"mandar"* (to command) are two things that indisputably the man does. That is why we speak of "the man's role" and "the woman's role": because, unlike most dances, in tango we have two different although coordinated choreographies for each member of "the couple." Obviously, I had failed, in the eyes of my circumstantial partner, to assume the basic role of "the man" for being unable "to command." So I knew I could not dance, not only because I intend to be a reasonable person but also because in the few attempts to dance in the *milongas* (in the real dances, not in the classes) I was almost immediately rejected. I also knew I could not dance because my *milonguero* "instincts" told me so.

That happened because I had learned to see myself just as anyone else on the dance floor would see me. With that, I had acquired that critical, sarcastic way of looking characteristic of my significant others. I could not do what was required of me on the dance floor, but I could recognize that in the actions of others and I had learned to recognize how they viewed my clumsy steps. With that, an important aspect of my natural relative conception of the world (namely, that all of us are unanimous, that as members we are all alike) was questioned.

The experience which made me aware of this distinction happened in one particular *milonga*. There, those who "cannot dance" do dance, and they are even the majority. In that *milonga*, I attended both the classes and then the dance. I also watched audacious young couples dance who made the dance floor their own, particularly on Fridays. But I did not feel a part of it because "that just isn't tango." I, who could not dance, somehow knew what it means to dance the Tango. Plus, I could recognize what those people were doing as strange ("not Tango") in that environment devoted to tourism and flirting but not so much to proper tango dancing. There I was allowed to dance, but my *milonguero* instincts made me feel an aversion to it. Of course, "instinct" is just a way to put it. It feels like instinctive behavior because it is not rational thinking but a global, emotional sense of the situation grasped perceptibly and shaped by past experiences sedimented which engender a perceptually based aesthetic that structures in its own fashion a taste of what is likeable and what is not. It is a kind of embodied sense of what "real tango" is. Well, because of that sense—which now I know constituted the natural worldview typical to any *tanguero*—I did not feel like dancing there, although I was allowed to.

The experiences just narrated faced me with ambiguous feelings. Am I or am I not a member of the *milonga*? A concern which, in turn, raised another question, prior and fundamental: What is it to be a member? An important aspect of my natural conception of the world as a member of the *milonga* had been already called into question. I had bracketed the idea that members might not be alike, that there can be substantial differences among them. This aspect of my natural conception of the world was challenged and new distinctions started to emerge. Which leads us to the second step of our method.

Once described and challenged by the natural attitude of a group, we proceed to describe its constancies by practicing a non-essentialist worldly analysis of essences. We aim at describing social facts in their regularities as the product of the coercive work of collective consciousness.

Back to our case study, I had noticed that the fact that I could not dance did not exclude me from the *milonga*. It just made me a particular kind of member: a member who "cannot dance." That was how I realized that the social setting of the *milonga* is partly organized on the base of negative certifications indicating who cannot dance. This opened the door for me to understanding the way the social setting of the *milonga* is structured.

One fundamental structuring factor is, indeed, the ability to dance. The simplest and basic distinction is, then, among those who "can dance" and those who cannot. So, not all members are alike, as I supposed before calling into question the natural attitude at the *milonga*. This is, in fact, the way members categorize each other, even if they are not totally aware of the consequences these categorization devices[8] have.

This members' categorization device differs from the one employed by tango teachers, who do not use two but three categories; namely, "beginners," "intermediate," and "advanced." So, the way ordinary dancers see each other partly diverges from the way teachers and assistants see students and practitioners. Even if both kinds of devices classify the same population (since most of the students stay late for the *milonga* and many of the dancers were or still are advanced students) and they both produce a similar hierarchy, whereby only those who can dance reach to the top, there are two main differences. First, the native categorization device is simpler: it only uses two categories ("can dance" / "cannot dance") in comparison to the professional device, which uses three ("beginners" / "intermediate" / "advanced"). Second, the divergences between both devices are stronger at the bottom than at the top. The professional device specifies two levels of non-competent members ("beginners" and "intermediate") while the native device only specifies one ("cannot dance"). However, they both acknowledge only one kind of fully competent member (those who "can dance" or who are "advanced" students). Furthermore, these higher categories include about the same population (usually who "can dance" is or was an "advanced" student).

Another structuring factor, which in turn is at the base of the factor just described, is the distinction between two different forms of membership with different reaches: "social competence," which is universal, and "technical competence," which is restricted. All who know what goes on in the *milongas*, who can assign meaning to the encounter of dancers and perceive the obvious as such, are competent members in the first sense. Only those who have incorporated bodily schemata through habits and achieved a personal synthesis of the historic *milonguero* style and a distinctive personal way of dance, are members in the second sense. The category of technically competent member is, and is expected to be, highly restricted. It implies aristocratic values with which the *milonga*'s community distinguishes "the best" dancers: those few members admired for their style, for their elegance, and for keeping alive "old fashioned tango" by renewing it through what in the future will be remembered as "this guy's style."

We must now account for the constitution of the worldly essences described so far by rendering observable the member's work, local methods, and autochthonous theorizing involved in the congregational labor of producing a local order. In other words, we must now practice sociological constitutional analysis. To that end, we should ask how those structural constancies are constituted by the group's congregational work.

The structuring of the population of *milongueros* described so far is a congregational accomplishment. In its production, members display a number of methodological resources by which they constitute, as a group, a given natural attitude. By becoming a member of the *milonga*, I got not only to see but, specially, to notice this cooperative work.

At the *milonga*, not everyone can dance. You must acquire the status of a dancer but of course you cannot give this to yourself, only others can give it to you. Experienced dancers and some regulars use to say, or whisper as if they were revealing a secret, that "so and so dances" when they want to acknowledge or point out someone's talent. But this is not just said about anyone.

Two main sets of methods are employed to assign status and produce social structures at the *milonga*, one used by ordinary members (practicants and dancers), which basically consists of informal techniques and tactics, another one, used by teachers and institutions to formally qualify and handle the congregation of *milongueros* which on a weekly or, even, a daily basis attend and economically support the *milongas* of Buenos Aires.

To understand the first kind of device, let us go back to the dance floor and to the moment where my partner was remarking my incompetence as a male dancer. In her eyes, I had failed to assume the basic role of "the man" for being unable "to command." Carrying out these functions on her own was proof that my partner judged me as incompetent. Since then, she avoided me on the dance floor for the rest of the night. Both things (pointing out someone's mistakes and avoiding dancing with her or him) are practical procedures that members use to decide that somebody cannot dance. It works as an ethnomethodological account. I got a lot of that. On the dance floor I was almost immediately rejected by women (usually with kind euphemisms like pretending there was someone waiting for them) and criticized by men (a few of them with a friendly attitude, as if they were giving me advice, the others with a tough attitude or even a sarcastic one). So, by pointing out my mistakes and by refusing to dance with me, my circumstantial partners were telling me that I could not dance.

The second kind of categorization device at the *milongas* aims at labeling and classify the congregation of practitioners. As already seen in this section, they are categorized into three levels: "Beginners," "Intermediates," and "Advanced." This categorization is a stratification based on the skills and competences acquired. The transition from one level to another occurs when the teacher thinks that the practitioner is competent enough (even in cases where promotion comes after the request and insistence of the person interested). There is not an exam but rather an ongoing evaluation.

Given that practitioners are classified according to their skills in two or three levels of increasing skills (according to who is categorizing), the whole set is based on the least competent stage, that is, on the "group" of those who "cannot dance" or who are "beginners." This is the largest group of all. Therefore, it makes an important contribution not only economically (as they are the majority of those who pay for the classes, drinks, and meals) but also to the whole dynamics of this social setting as it is the one that provides a substantial number of members. It can be said that the incompetence of a large number of members is essential for the functioning of dance classes and, given its closeness to the *milonga*, it also helps to enhance it. Accordingly, it is important to describe how the incompetence of the many is routinely produced as a condition of the competence of the few.

Much of its production happens during the tango classes. Contrary to how people learned to dance tango in the old times (spontaneously and guided by friends and acquaintances rather than "teachers"), nowadays its learning is mediated by professional instructors, it is systematized by a set of teaching techniques, and, above all, it is institutionalized so that, except in a few exceptional cases, they are run as academies rather than as mere dance halls. This makes it possible to categorize in a standardized way the population of trainees into three different levels and to distinguish a few sanctioned dancers from all the rest.

As a result, the class is nowadays an annex of the dance floor. What is most common is that it starts before the *milonga* begins so that those who are competent enough can first practice and then dance. This also adds an extra public as quite a few beginners, and even curious companions, stay as spectators and participants in the social life of the *milonga*—which of course involves buying a drink or even having dinner there. So nowadays, classes and *milongas* usually work in conjunction with one another.

In this context, the class is organized in a collection of practitioners based on their competences where the "teacher" knows the competences and incompetences of each student and addresses the class in general, interacting with each of the levels separately and with all of them together.

Since in both categorization devices only a few make it to the top, the technical incompetence of the many supports the continued production of the exceptional competence of the few. Indeed, the category of technical competence in tango dance is deliberately built to be exclusive. It is known that the vast majority will never reach it, which condemns us to the role of mere spectators.

There is a moment in the *milonga* where all but two people are spectators: it is "show time." Every *milonga*—particularly at peak times—have starring dance partners. It is known that "today so and so dancers are performing." This creates expectations among the people there. When the dance is at its peak, the floor empties, theater lights (where available) are switched on and everybody watches from their tables or stands on the edge of the dance floor while the starring couple dances a few tangos. This moment marks the distinction between the two meanings of membership in the *milonga*: those "who can dance" and those who, as spectators, consecrate the exceptional virtuosity of the most eminent members of the tango scene.

Considered as a whole, these methods produce the heterogeneity of the social settings of the *milongas*. In the last analysis, my research disclosed a structural inequality. Social settings are heterogeneous and precisely require this heterogeneity to exist. Thus, they can be described according to their degree of internal diversity. Some competences are accessible to all members; therefore, they can be universalized and distributed homogeneously among them. Some others are specifics and difficult to acquire; therefore, they are distributed heterogeneously.

Heterogeneity can take different forms. In my research, I explored the heterogeneity between social and specialized competences, which makes it possible for some members to significantly interact within certain social settings although they have different competencies. The first type of competences is potentially available to any member, the second type is fully achieved only by a few exceptional members—they fall outside of the ordinary and therefore are prohibitive to most members. So, technical competencies dismantle the unity of understanding and action, meaning and practice, which characterizes ordinary memberships. Accordingly, these two forms of membership have different reaches: social competence is universal, technical competence is restricted. This makes meaningful the expression "incompetent members," since not all socially competent members are technically competent.

CONCLUSIONS

In this chapter, we have seen how phenomenological sociology proceeds—not how it should proceed but how it actually does. The distinction is important. Telling how a discipline should proceed is aiming at founding a new field of research. That was not at all my aim. Instead, telling how a discipline has been proceeding along the last two centuries (namely, from Durkheim on) is claiming that, as a matter of fact, it exists. Indeed, having disclosed a long-term practice of the phenomenological method in sociology (even if not all practitioners were fully aware of that), this chapter has contributed to establish as a matter of fact the existence of a phenomenological sociology, which—as seen in the introduction—was called into question by many scholars.

The method of phenomenological sociology can be put in a few words, once considered the reasons and illustrations provided in this chapter. It starts not with the performance of the *epoché* but with the description of an *epoché* already performed in groups. We do not bracket anything on our own but rather disclose what everybody brackets as members of a given group. After describing—this means, after having circumscribed topically—the natural attitude of a group, we can describe its constancies. We proceed then to do worldly eidetic analysis, whose object is to describe social facts in their regularities as produced by the coercive work of collective consciousness. Once established these "non essentialistic essences," we proceed to account for their constitution by rendering observable the member's work, local methods and autochthonous theorizing involved in the congregational labor of producing a local order. Describing these collective accomplishments is the central task of constitutional analysis in phenomenological sociology.

There are many other ways to practice phenomenology in the social sciences (applied phenomenology, qualitative research, etc.). Nevertheless, the paradigm described by Psahtas, which launched the intellectual movement of phenomenological sociology (as argued in the introduction), requires more than just taking ideas from phenomenological philosophy and applying them in social research. It requires, among other things, a specific method. Therefore, describing the idea and the actual use of that method is an important step toward the systematization and rationalization of phenomenological sociology.

The need to disclose the use of the phenomenological method in sociology comes from centuries of oblivion. Its use has long been neglected, even for some of its users. However, their pre-reflexive practice has been crucial for us in establishing a way to proceed in accordance with a long-held practical tradition.

This tradition may well benefit from approaching other perspectives. I am not claiming that this is the only method valid in social sciences nor that every phenomenological sociologist must limit himself to apply these few steps. I am just saying that the practical use of the phenomenological method in sociology has been used for a very long time and must be considered as a congregational work. Briefly, all I am saying is that we, phenomenological sociologists, exist.

NOTES

1. Barber mentions numerous cases, such as "the spatial loci of cabarets, coffee houses, the *Opéra Comique*, Las Vegas comedy theaters, the commedia dell'arte, and the temporal periods of the Dionysian and Saturnalian cults, carnaval and Mardi Gras (celebrated the day before Ash Wednesday in Christianity), the Feast of Fools (celebrated in the medieval era by lower clergy to mock society's upper echelon), April Fool's Day, the Hindu Holi celebrations (every spring), the hour-and-a-half Saturday Night Live television performances in the United States, and various celebrations of fools (e.g., Islam's Nasredden)" (Barber 2017, 182).

2. For a phenomenological critique of racism, see Gordon (2000, 72–80, and Gordon 2008, 79).

3. Durkheim not only performs eidetic analysis but also the phenomenological reduction (see Belvedere 2015a).

4. "The misreading consisted of learning as sociology's relevant enterprise to discard not only Gestalt theory and Gestalt principles as these were respecified by Gurwitsch's transcendental phenomenological researches. Gurwitsch's respecified generics of *Gestalt* theory and principles consisted of generics based on line drawings, lecture, and laboratory demonstrations" (Garfinkel 2002, 258).

5. On the Schutzian concept of the cultural sciences, see Embree (2015).

6. It was Psathas who brilliantly conceived the idea that Garfinkel's ethnomethodology must be considered as an experimentation with the natural attitude. I expand on this in a paper published in his honor (Belvedere 2020).

7. *Milonga* is slang from Buenos Aires. It has many different meanings, most of which are beside the point. In this paper, I will use *milonga* as "tango dance halls," and *milonguero* as "tango dancer" or "tango fan."

8. Membership Categorization Devices "are collections of categories for referring to persons, with some rules of application" that members apply to populations to say things about them and which they "use together or collect together" as a set, i.e., as "categories-that-go-together" (Sacks 1995, 238).

Chapter Four

Some Fundamental Findings in Phenomenological Sociology

The aim of this chapter is to present—in an integrated, systematic perspective—the most important findings in phenomenological sociology. To the mainstream sociologist these might seem "theoretical claims." They are not. They are not the product of general thinking but the result of in-depth descriptions produced and collected along the years in the bosom of the Schutzian tradition. Of course, this wealth of treasures will be exposed in my own way, from a perspective irredeemably mine. However, nothing else than its exposition is personal. Its content belongs to the history of phenomenological sociology.

Six topics will be addressed; namely, the *ego agens* considered as the substratum of social life, *pragmata* as this ego's positing acts, habitualities as the result of the reiterableness of *pragmata* and as acquisitions of the ego, social personalities as originating in the split of the *ego agens* in a multiplicity of partial selves, and institutions as standardized patterns of social behavior. However, these are not isolated items. On the contrary, they form a gradient going from the first distinction between the personal and the social—which is to be found in the split of temporality in *durée* (or inner time) and public time—all the way through to the most impersonal forms of social behavior, which are objectified, reified and mystified. This will show that behavior can take different forms, subjective as well as objective, because it can experience a wide range of transformations thanks to specific qualities of *pragmata* such as reiterableness and tranferability.

THE MONAD AS THE *HYPOKEIMENON*
OF SOCIAL LIFE

In chapter 1, I argue that Schutz practiced egology even if he used the word
scarcely. This has not only a philosophical but also a sociological import
since many of his "analyses of the modes of givenness of social phenomena
proceeded in an egological perspective" (Eberle 2012, 288).

In the following, I will focus on five of these social phenomena which
find their substratum or *hypokeimenon* in the monad (or concrete ego), which
Schutz conceives as an *ego ipse*; namely: *pramata,* habitualities, social personalities, social roles, and social institutions. To that end, I will argue that the
concrete ego is the subject who constitutes and enacts all social phenomena.
As Schutz claims, "the relevant index to the social person" is to be found in
the *ego agens* conceived as "*a pragmatic* unification" (Schutz 2013, 209) and
as "the *origo* of pure pragma" (Schutz 2013, 210).[1]

In Schutz's view, "the actor qua actor [. . .] is subject, substance, monad"
(Schutz 2013, 219). The social is a set of social personalities orientated
"around the *ego* agens" (Schutz 2013, 224), which he conceives as being
partial, fragmentary, and even "schizophrenic" (Schutz 2013, 249). Giving
its relevance for phenomenological sociology, let us take a closer look to
Schutz's ideas on the subject as monad and its relation to social personalities.

The monad is a "subjective experiencing of temporality"—that is, a "constituted immanence" (Schutz 2013, 265). This constituted immanence is in
turn "a constituting moment for the stratification of the self" through a series
of modifications of the "pure pragma of the self at work" (Schutz 2013, 265).
The *ego agens* is the self "working on its pragma, [which] is always the *ego
ipse* in its totality and fullness" (Schutz 2013, 270).

Schutz's claim is that we must start from the concrete ego as the substratum
of what sociological theory calls "the actor" since the difference between
objective and subjective meaning is rooted in the different ways in which
an Ego-consciousness configures meaning (Schutz 1967, 40). Furthermore,
the distinction between the concepts of action and act is based in meaning-
constitution processes of internal time-consciousness because "all action
takes place in time, or more precisely in the internal time-consciousness,
in the *durée*. It is duration-immanent enactment. Act, on the other hand, is
duration transcendent enactedness" (Schutz 1967, 40). Thus, the ultimate cri-
terium used to distinguish between objective and subjective meaning and to
distinguish the actor as a real person and as a theoretical construct is one and
the same: both pairs of concepts must be considered in their relation to actual
processes of meaning constitution in the inner time of the Ego. Moreover,
any type of behavior "presupposes an activity of the Ego" whose meaning is

established "in Acts wherein the Ego takes up one attitude or position after another" (Schutz 1962, 41). Indeed, meaning-endowing experiences "must rather be an 'Ego-Act' (attitudinal Act) or some modification of such an Act (secondary passivity, or perhaps a passively emerging judgment that suddenly 'occurs to me')" (Schutz 1962, 54).

In continuity with these considerations, the genesis of *pragmata*, habitualities, social personalities, social roles, and institutions shall find its basis in meaning-constitution processes of the ego.

PRAGMA IN EGOLOGICAL PERSPECTIVE

Within this framework, Schutz claims that "the general positing of the *ego agens*" is the "*origo* of pure *pragma*" (Schutz 2013, 210). More precisely, he states that the origin of the pure *pragma* lies in "a general positing '*of my* acting self' [that] corresponds to the general positing of the *alter ego* (which is a general positing of the *alter ego cogitans*)" (Schutz 2013, 209).

Schutz developed "a theory of the complete pragma" which can be systematized as a set of four features. First, *pragmata* rely on a general positing act. Second, this positing is related to duration since *pragmata* are acts of a self. Therefore, *pragmata* are experiencings in our *durée* (Schutz 2013, 209). Yet *pragmata* are not just any act in our *durée* but one in which the self is "founded in duration *acts* in the external world and accordingly gears into world-time" (Schutz 2013, 209). Third, *pragmata* must gear into the world. Fourth and last, *pragmata* are sedimented experiences "accomplished *by me*" (Schutz 2013, 226). Concisely, *pragmata* are sedimented experiences accomplished by the *ego* as positing acts of its *durée* geared into the external world.

Although action is a kind of *pragma*, not any kind of *pragma* is a rational, projected action. Schutz makes it clear:

> We do not speak of "acting" [*Handeln*], because the term is also involved with an inner attitude [*Einstellung*]. Instead we explicitly speak of "working," accordingly of the execution of the pragma in bodily movement itself, of the engagement of the self in world-space and in world-time by the changing of places by the body or its parts. (Schutz 2013, 276–277)

Bodily movements in space are clear-cut examples of *pragma*—for instance, a change of place (Schutz 2013, 227) "by virtue of which an *illic* becomes a *hic*" (Schutz 2013, 286). On the contrary, reflective, theorizing acts are "*pragma*-free actions" because "they are not bound to working in the external world" (Schutz 2013, 231). So, there can be *pragmata* which are not actions as well as *pragmata*-free actions. Moreover, only one out of four types of *pragma* is related to action, as can be seen by taking a closer look to Schutz's stratification of them.

Schutz's concept of *pragma* is articulated into four *strata*: (a) the *pragma* without the purpose and project; (b) the *pragma* with the purpose but without the project; (c) the *pragma* with the project and purpose; and (d) the *pragma* with the project but without the purpose.

In this perspective, only *pragma* with the project and purpose is rational acting. So, *pragma* is both more and less than rational action: it is more because it covers a wider range than action, and it is less because—exception made of the *pragma* with the project and purpose—it has fewer requirements because it does not need to be consciously aware of the end (purpose), nor its need to pursue it, neither to know about the adequate means to achieve it. What is more, Schutz believed that the first kind of *pragma* (without the purpose and the project) does not even need to be intentional.

Schutz developed these ideas further, explicitly distinguishing "conscious *pragma*" from "unconscious *pragma*." Conscious *pragma* is not only intentional but also directed to a purpose, whereas unconscious pragma "lacks purpose as well as project." Based on such distinction, Schutz renames the first type of pragma—which he formerly called "mere reaction" or "mere behavior"—as "unconscious *pragma*." Of course, unconscious *pragma* is what he meant by mere behavior, but we know now that it lacks the specific feature of conscious *pragma*: the intended purpose. Afterward, Schutz speaks of habitual behaving as the second type of pragma, that is, the "empirical behavior." Although we do not have a new name for this, it is enlightening to know that this kind of *pragma* refers to habitualities since (as will be seen later) they play a main role in the genesis of the social person. It is even more interesting to note that Schutz calls the third kind of pragma "action in the full sense," confirming what he had said about the *pragma* with the project and purpose.

Yet, the specification of *actio* as a kind of *pragma* poses one question. If the subject of social actions is the actor, which is the subject of *pragma*? To address this question, we need to retrieve Schutz's egology since his answer is that the subject who performs the *pragma* is the concrete *ego* or monad as a "subjective experiencing of temporality"—i.e., as a "constituted immanence"—and, in turn, as "a constituting moment for the stratification of the self" through a series of modifications of the "pure *pragma* of the self at work" (Schutz 2013, 265).

As the pure pragma is constituent of the self at work, the *ego agens* is always the self "working on its *pragma*." This is what Schutz calls "the *ego ipse* in its totality and fullness" (Schutz 2013, 270). As such, it is a present self, actually working, and only this self at work "is the core of reality of the surrounding world, the actual world within reach" (Schutz 2013, 284).

Hence, the *ego agens* as the *ego ipse* in its totality and fullness is the self now that operates and "creates its public time while operating" (Schutz 2013, 270). All the other "basic attitudes of the self, comprised under the headings of 'interest' and 'attention,' [. . .] are themselves pragmatically conditioned, i.e., are modifications of that *attention à la vie* originating in the pure pragma of the self at work" (Schutz 2013, 265).

Such kinds of attitudes—which are modifications of the pure pragma— "modify the experiences of expectation and of memory that arise from reflection on the course of duration" and "these ramifications can be traced back to the frames of spatio-temporality constituted in the 'daily life' [. . . where] no self is simply given but always given in need of a temporal index. It is the self now, the self before now, and the self later on," which Schutz calls the "*tempora* of the self" (Schutz 2013, 265).

In this perspective, the *ego agens* (while *ego ipse* in its totality and fullness) operates as my self now by constituting its *actiones* as *pragmata* and simultaneously co-constituting public time as "split up into a piece of world-time in which the *acta* have taken place in a sequential order of succession and in flowing duration and which my *acta* have constituted" (Schutz 2013, 270). Briefly, public time "is created by my *pragma* in the process of execution" (Schutz 2013, 270). Consequently, every *actio* is made up of two different but related phenomena: on one hand, it is "a series of experiencings in duration"; on the other, it is a "working (*pragma*) in world-time" (Schutz 2013, 209).

All this occurs in the present. Even though my self before has operated in the past, it does not operate now. That is why I think about its *actiones* "only as its *acta*." As *actiones,* these *pragmata* are co-constituting of the public time which was the complete "Now" for the previously operating self, but to me, as reflecting self, appear as "then" emergent within the frame of public time (Schutz 2013, 270).

THE REITERABLENESS OF *PRAGMA* AND
THE GENESIS OF HABITUALITIES

Only *pragmata* accomplished by "my self now" can be said to be actual and real. On the contrary, *pragmata* accomplished by "my self before" are characterized as potential and, consequently, as a "reality in the mode of probability" derived from an "earlier core of reality" (Schutz 2013, 226). Accordingly, the "reiterableness" of the same *pragma* and of an analogous *pragma* by my self later on is "contained in the idealization of 'I always can again'" (Schutz 2013, 226). One could think that this reiterableness not only allows for the development of personal habits but also for the establishing of a social *habitus*[2] since *pragmata* are reiterable not only by the *ego agens* that created them but also by other *egos*. That is why Schutz depicts them as reiterable *and* analogous.

Schutz not only distinguishes actual from potential *pragmata* but also two different levels of potentiality. The first level is the one of "the previously actual *pragma* that potentially is reiterable" (Schutz 2013, 228). It is "the world of 'phenomena of probability,'" which corresponds to "the full reality of the surrounding world in the extent of its reach" (Schutz 2013, 228). Although, these "phenomena of probability which previously stood in the surrounding world of the core of reality" refer not only to the actual world of "my self now": they also "refer back to my prior self for which it was the core of reality" (Schutz 2013, 284).

> In so far as the level of the first potentiality lies within the range of the actual projects of the self at work, the phenomena attributed to the self belong to my self now. But that is also to say that the reiterability of working under the pragmatic ideality of "one can always again" bears in this case the character of greatest probability. For this level of first potentiality it is characteristic that the protentions directed to the reactualization of the *pragma* obtain their intentionalities from reproductions and retentions of their own receding pragmas. (Schutz 2013, 284–285)

Accordingly, the *attention à la vie*, which in the purely actual *pragma* is "limited to my self now," is here "extended to my self later on, however always related back to my previous self" (Schutz 2013, 228).[3] This sort of extension makes possible that "protentions procure their intentionalities from reproductions and retentions of pragmas that have receded into the past" (Schutz 2013, 228) and thus it is a sine qua non condition for the reiterability of *pragmata* (Schutz 2013, 228).

The second level of potentiality is the one of "potential *pragma*," which is "always stemming from the level of the *ego ipse*" and whose boundaries "lie only in the compatibility and compossibility of the in-order-to motives, of the projects, of specific relations of ends or means with the whole experience, especially with respect to the experience of one's own pragma, its practicability and "its own powers" (Schutz 2013, 228). Schutz describes it as "the level of the world in reachability" and as "quite different in structure" in comparison with the first level: it is "a level of the reality of future working" (Schutz 2013, 285). As such, it "belongs to my later self, at the most to my self itself later on and is without an essential relation back to my prior self. It is then the case that, like all anticipations, it is founded in the actual stock of experience of my self now which, for its part, genetically refers back to my prior self" (Schutz 2013, 285).

This retro-reference of the actual self to its prior self occurs partially in the inner flow of consciousness. Husserl was attentive to this. In his view—which enriches Schutz's observations on this matter—any act occurs in the temporal flow of consciousness and, if it has a new objective meaning, the "I" acquires a new property that will be maintained permanently, not only as something remembered but also as something that "has been." The I can always return to that property numerous times and always finds it there for him as his own, as an acquisition of his habitus (Martínez 2007, 148). This is important for understanding how the habitus work.

For Husserl, the habitus is the mediator between the passive "already there" and the activity of knowledge, and it constitutes the sedimentations of the life-world's *doxic* soil (Martínez 2007, 150). Consequently, it is the passive synthesis that which is presented to the ego in the form of a *habitus* and thus that which encompasses the work of the active synthesis (Martínez 2007, 149).

In this light, the habitus is seen as an acquisition of the concrete persistent personal ego, constituted in its temporalization. In other words, the habitus is an egoic persistent substratum of egoic qualities. Therefore, it always pertains to an ego which persists, as a person, through the changes of his habitus, and who grows habitual properties (Husserl 2006, 41).

We may say then that the "substratum of habitualities" is the ego (Husserl 2006, 92). The genesis of the ego's persistent properties is to be found in the constitution, in the flowing intentional life, of a surrounding world of objects endowed with their horizons and permanent ways of being and being-so (Husserl 2006, 91). The ego is always surrounded by objects which affect it and incite it to action. Habitus is what makes the world already available always there for the I (Martínez 2007, 149). Thus, habituality is the correlate of the positing of these objects constituted in the I pole which performs them (Husserl 2006, 91). This is how a habituality is constituted, and once constituted it pertains also to the constitution of objects existing there for the I, so that it is always possible to go back to it again and again (Husserl 2006, 103–104).

These objects exist for me in my surrounding world in which I find both objects that are already familiar to me with a permanent organization and objects whose knowledge is only anticipated by me. The first ones are there for me by an original acquisition (i.e., due to an originary act of positing and specification in particular intuitions of things I have never seen). This kind of object is constituted, throughout my synthetic activity, in the explicit meaning form of what is identical to itself, determined by its many properties. My activity of positing and specifying the being establishes a habituality of my own by which this object becomes permanently of my property as an object with its own determinations. Such permanent acquisitions constitute my own known surrounding world with its horizon of unknown objects, that is, still to be acquired, but already anticipated in its formal object-like structure (Husserl 2006, 91–92).

As we can see, Husserl focuses not just on the habitus but on the ego's habitus. Consequently, he never loses sight of the fact that it is always the ego endowed with the habitus and not the habitus by itself who acts. By doing so, he takes as the basis of phenomenological sociology the concrete personal ego in a concrete situation, related to concrete others. In this light, the habitus is seen as an acquisition of men in a concrete situation and in social relationships, which are habitual associations of a habitual "we," whose habitualities belong to them in a particular way.

ALL OF MY SELVES AND THE GENESIS
OF SOCIAL PERSONALITIES

As seen in the previous section, the experience of the ego's *pragma* is dependent on the experience of one's own powers. This means that human powers are always, in the most radical sense, powers of an *ego*. However, the ego contains not only its own powers but also the index to the social persons.

> The "self *per se*" is *a pragmatic* unification: *ego agens et semper idem agens* (*volens*). In this context, *agens* as *self* contains as well, to be sure, the relevant index to the social person (*ego* qua *pater familias,* qua *civis Romanus,* (*iaphilosophus,* etc.). As a consequence, all of these modifications are shown to be precisely modifications of the one *ego* ipse *agens* (volens) (appearing in the general positing of the *ego agens* as *origo* of pure *pragma*). (Schutz 2013, 209–210)

The *ego agens* is surrounded by a stratification of social persons based on the "split of temporality" between *durée* and cosmic time originating from "the subjective experiencing of temporality as constituting immanence" (Schutz 2013, 220), which is stratified "into my self now, my self before now, my self later on" (Schutz 2013, 221).

Thus, social persons are based on "the subjective experiencing of temporality as constituting immanence" (Schutz 2013, 220) which, in turn, is "the situation in its original fullness" and "the basic attitude of *attention à la vie* in the solitary self" (Schutz 2013, 238). My acting self, "the *ego ipse agens* is constituted at the same time as the center of working (the center of action) from which all habitualities and automaticities take their departure" (Schutz 2013, 279). Thereafter, through habituality (as well as through will, sociality, education, and culture), an interdependence and hierarchy of *attentions à la vie* is formed (Schutz 2013, 239). In accordance, the new levels of personality become "eccentric from the levels of personality that until now were central" and, in the reverse process, potentialities that have become eccentric "can become central again or devolve into 'partial death'" (Schutz 2013, 239).

The "orientation of all other personalities around the *ego agens*" (Schutz 2013, 224) produces a stratification of the self (Schutz 2013, 265) arranged in "a continuous transition from the absolutely intimate person to the highest anonymous behavior" (Schutz 2013, 236). While "only *actio* creates a unity of relations" and is "ascribed to the unitary *ego ipse*," *acta* are to be ascribed "to partial social persons" which are constituted in the sedimentation of these *acta* (Schutz 2013, 221).

The stratifications of social personalities around the self are not only synchronic but also diachronic. The different *tempora* of the self, open the horizons (past, present, and future) of all possible *pragma*. As a pragmatic unification, the *ego ipse* is produced in the Now, which provides for it the opportunity

> to come into view in its fullness and totality as an operative [*wirkendes*] self in its *actio,* while my self before now is already split up into its partial aspects and can never be visible in its fullness and totality but always only in its partial aspect. For only the *actio* creates the relationship of unity [*Einheitsbezug*] of the *ego ipse* [. . .] Only the self now operates so as to be able to achieve this production [*Leistung*] of the relationship of unity. (Schutz 2013, 271)

Unlike my self now, my self before now does not operate but has already operated. That is why it does not create the unification of my *ego ipse,* although its *acta* are constitutive of my past, partial self. In Schutz's words:

> My self before now does not operate, it *has* operated and its *acta* do not become allotted to the unitary *ego* ipse. Rather they are already revealed as *acta* of a partial self. Indeed, we can say right away that each of the partial selves which, in retrospect, make up my self before now, are nothing else than my *acta* constituting each of the partial selves such that I allot them specific attitudes of myself. (Schutz 2013, 271)

For Schutz, "to allot" means that the reproduction of my partial selves' *acta* "results in specific attentional, and, for their part, new pragmatically conditioned modifications, thus sedimented [*geschichtet*] according to hypsographical contour lines of relevance the center of density of which likewise lies in my self now" (Schutz 2013, 271).

So, my self now is the center of all my partial social persons, constituted through the sedimentation of my *pragmata*. Some of these "partial persons of my self are referred to as belonging to my self now," while others, whose aspects "belong just to Now, bear the marks of the self later on—all of this to be sure only when in its totality the *ego ipse* does not presentively realize them in an actual *pragma*" (Schutz 2013, 273–274).

Besides, actual *pragmata* performed by my self now are phenomenologically real, while past and future *pragmata* remain or await in the horizons for my actual working self. This means that each *tempora* of the self has its own peculiar features. While it is essential to my self now and my self later on to constitute public time—along with its postestativeness, its possibility, and "its possibility of freely calculating probability and freely choosing among probabilities" (Schutz 2013, 271)—it is proper of my self before now to be complete, i.e., unchangeable and irrecoverable, because it "is no longer postestative and no long allows for a choice" since "I no longer have the choice of what I will have done" (Schutz 2013, 271).

As far as I find my *pragmata* in the Before—which "is free of protentions and anticipations"—"they are reproducible or retainable as experiences of duration" and "carry their horizons open with them because they belong to my actual duration" though, "in so far as my self before now belongs to world-time, there no longer are no protentions and anticipations in a genuine and original sense because my previous protentions and anticipations have either been fulfilled or unfulfilled" (Schutz 2013, 271). This is why "the acts which have entered into my world-time are as they are, unique, unchangeable and can no longer be freely varied" (Schutz 2013, 271).

On the contrary, my present *pragmata*—performed by my self now as "the completed synthesis in public time of the present *pragma*"—have their "open and undetermined, freely variable protentions and anticipations" which are "protentions and anticipations-now that carry with them a maximal probability of fulfillment" (Schutz 2013, 271).

The later on, in turn, "simply remains undecided and open" while in the "genuine past" there are "only completion and certainty" (Schutz 2013, 271). Indeed, when it comes to the self later on, "the ideas of the future self accompanying protentions and anticipations are unfulfilled and remain essentially unfulfillable from the standpoint of Now" (Schutz 2013, 274), as it is "universally the case of all expectations and also all phantasies whose transport into reality, whose realization, as we say, is not excluded beforehand" (Schutz 2013, 274).

As mentioned before, the sedimentation of my *acta* constitutes my different partial selves allotted with specific attitudes (Schutz 2013, 271). These attitudes are partial personalities orientated around the *ego agens* and constituted by "habitualities and their automatisms" (Schutz 2013, 224) by virtue of the transferability of one's own pragmata (Schutz 2013, 285).

Also, they do not exist disconnectedly but compose a system "defined by our attitudes toward the different phenomena of the social world" (Schutz 2013, 247). It is "a system of interconnections of motivations" simply accepted "as habitual, traditional or affective givennesses" (Schutz 2013, 247).

This system of attitudes is given in diverse ways, starting from standardized normative attitudes in the cultural world of daily life, moving on to "the ultimate goals of our bearing on the great systems of the state, of the law, of the economy—in short, all of those phenomena of social being that form the specific object of the social sciences" (Schutz 2013, 248).

Accordingly, habitualities play an important role in the constitution and stabilization of the system of our social attitudes. The more habitualized and rationalized the different levels of the social person are, the more visible they become (Schutz 2013, 238). In turn, this process of stabilization is based on common knowledge since it retrieves apprehensions of the world which, as such, always refer back

> to the stock of experience which the self previously constructed out of multiple polythetic and monothetic concatenations of meaning already contained in previous experiences. And also belonging to this stock of experience in principle are the memories of modifications which the cores of reality of the previous surrounding world have undergone by *acts of genuine working.* (Schutz 2013, 282, Schutz's emphasis)

In addition, "what can be anticipated as the reality of future working must [. . .] be compossible with this actual stock of experience" (Schutz 2013, 285), which involves "experiencings of my own pragma, of its 'transferability' (actualizableness) and thus the 'estimation of its own power'" (Schutz 2013, 285).

Based on these estimations, I can work in the world within reach, which is related to my self later on, and accordingly "remains subject to the double concurrence of probability which is universally characteristic for my self later on" (Schutz 2013, 285).

SOCIAL PERSONALITIES AND SOCIAL ROLES

According to express indications of Schutz, the phenomenological basis of the genesis of social roles must be found in his observations on the *ego agens* and on social personalities given in his manuscripts of 1936 and 1937 (in Schutz 2013). Seen this way, roles and role expectations are parts of social personalities (Spiegelberg 1980, 171), and the ways in which they are interpreted form a part of the core of the personality that we call "the *self*" (Mitchell 2000, 151). Let us now take a look at how Schutz elaborates on this idea.

Schutz's conception of social roles[4] starts with the hypothesis of the schizophrenic ego as partitioned into multiple social personalities. This *ego*, which is a pragmatic unification, determines which factors of its personality must operate in a certain area of the social world and therefore which role it will assume and its positioning in a more or less central stratum of its personality. Seen this way, social roles are attitudes that, in our daily lives, "we voluntarily assume as expedients and which we may drop whenever we want to do so" (Schutz 1964, 82). Although social constituents such as the social stock of knowledge play a significant part in structuring social roles, they also involve "a self-typification on the part of the incumbent" (Schutz 1964, 237) as they are "existential elements" of the situation that he has "to take into account" and with which he has "to come to terms" (Schutz 1964, 250). Therefore, it is an error "to identify the self with its roles" (Storm Heter 2006, 19), "since no individual can define a social role alone, [and] role awareness requires understanding the institutional dimension of the role, for example the common social expectations regarding the rights and responsibilities of the role" (Storm Heter 2006, 27). Thus, social roles have both subjective and objective meaning.

For the above said, Schutz considered the concept of role an element of a network of typifications of human individuals, of their course-of-action patterns, of their motives and goals, and of the sociocultural products which originated in their actions. These types were formed in the main by others, his predecessors or contemporaries, as appropriate tools for coming to terms with things and men, accepted as such by the group into which he was born. There are also self-typifications: man typifies to a certain extent his own situation within the social world and the various relations he has to his fellow men and cultural objects (Schutz 1964, 232–233). In other words, "role" and "role expectations" are elements of the social stock of knowledge.

The ability to typify and self-typify, to define roles and role expectations, originates in a particularity of the spiritual subject rooted

> in the fact that within it the apperception "I" emerges, in which apperception this "subject" is the "object" (although not always the thematic object). We have therefore to distinguish "I who I am" on the subjective side, and "I who I am" as object for me, the Me, which is in a specific sense represented, constituted, eventually intended within the being "I am." Under the Me we understand the person, constituted for me, the I which is conscious as a Self. (Schutz 1966, 32)

By virtue of this ability to self-constitute, the individual can choose which attitude to adopt toward the role he plays in the group. Accordingly, his role-playing is, to some extent, "one aspect of the private definition of the individual's membership situation" (Schutz 1964, 253). Therefore, we have to distinguish "the objective meaning of the social role and the role expectation as defined by the institutionalized pattern," from "the particular subjective way in which the incumbent of this role defines his situation within it" (Schutz 1964, 253).

From the incumbent's point of view, social roles are self-typifications. In Schutz's, words: "in the individual's definition of his private situation the various social roles originating in his multiple membership in numerous groups are experienced as a set of self-typifications which in turn are arranged in a particular private order of domains of relevances that is, of course, continuously in flux" (Schutz 1964, 254). This has consequences not only for the individual (who is to some extent free to define the role he will assume) but also for the ways he is considered within the group. For instance, not everything relevant to him is relevant to the group.

> It is possible that exactly those features of the individual's personality which are to him of the highest order of relevance are irrelevant from the point of view of any system of relevances taken for granted by the group of which he is a member. This may lead to conflicts within the personality, mainly originating in the endeavor to live up to the various and frequently inconsistent role expectations inhering in the individual's membership in various social groups. (Schutz 1964, 254)

Even if Schutz enhances the role played by the individual actor in the definition of roles, his stance is not individualistic. For sure, I can "use my self as a model of what others who perform this role are like, i.e., what the world is as seen by typical others from this perspective" (Psathas 1968, 519). Not to mention that the individual is always a member of a group and identifies a role and its position in relation to roles of the group through a system of typifications and relevances shared with others.

It is precisely "this acceptance of a common system of relevances" what "leads the members of the group to a homogenous self-typification" (Schutz 1964, 252) by means of a socialization process that involves as a significant aspect the learning of various markings and indications for "the position, status, role, and prestige each individual occupies or has within the stratification of the group" (Schutz and Luckmann 1989, 290).

In fact, to find his bearings in the group, the individual must be aware of different ways of behaving and must learn to distinguish between "the manifold badges, insignias, and emblems which are approved by the group as indicating social status and therefore as socially relevant" (Schutz and Luckmann 1989, 290). They determine which typical behaviors, actions, and motives one may expect from another person according to his or her position, status, role, and degree of prestige. Typical social roles and behavioral expectations of those who assume these roles must also be identified to play the corresponding appropriate role and to engage in behavior met with social approval from the group (Schutz and Luckmann 1989, 290).

Thus, it is a system of relevances and typifications that which "transforms unique individual actions of unique human beings into typical functions of typical social roles, originating in typical motives aimed at bringing about typical ends" (Schutz 1964, 237). Thus, "the incumbent of a social role is expected by the other members of the ingroup to act in the typical way defined by this role" (Schutz 1964, 237). Nonetheless, "by living up to his role the incumbent typifies himself; that is, he resolves to act in the typical way defined by the social role he has assumed. [. . .] Any role thus involves a self-typification on the part of the incumbent" (Schutz 1964, 237).

In addition, the different characteristics of groups allow for different levels of individual autonomy. It is worth mentioning that some groups allow for more freedom than others to determine from a personal point of view the features of social roles and the ways in which they are assumed. Specifically,

> it is only with respect to voluntary, and not to existential group membership, that the individual is free to determine [. . .] of which social role therein [in the group] he wants to be the incumbent. It is, however, at least one aspect of freedom of the individual that he may choose for himself with which part of his personality he wants to participate in group memberships; that he may define his situation within the role of which he is the incumbent. (Schutz 1964, 254)

Schutz (1964, 250) accepts the well-known sociological classification of voluntary and involuntary groups (which he also refers to as "existential groups"). As a member of an existential group, the individual must assume his social role as an "existential element" of the situation that he must take into account and with which he has to come to terms (Schutz 1964, 250). Instead, as a member of a voluntary group, he can choose to partake in it or not, and to some extent he has the freedom to choose which roles he will assume (Schutz 1964, 250).

As noted above, social roles require more than individual choices. It is relevant that they also entail holding a particular set of expectations that anyone who assumes them must fulfill. In Schutz's terminology,

> these role expectations are nothing but typifications of interaction patterns which are socially approved ways of solving typical problems and are frequently institutionalized. Consequently, they are arranged in domains of relevances

which in turn are ranked in a particular order originating in the group's relative natural conception of the world, its folkways, mores, morals, etc. (Schutz 1964, 269)

As part of the relative natural conception of the world, social roles are "located ahead of the social group," which holds this worldview as (a) "a component of socially approved type-formation," (b) "a store of socio-culturally derived knowledge that is usually communicated traditionally," (c) "standardized forms of the stock of knowledge with predesignated relevance structures whose conformity is warranted by genetic socialization," (d) and "type-formations" that can even "lead to institutionalization" (Schutz and Luckmann 1989, 212).

SOCIAL INSTITUTIONS AS STANDARDIZED PATTERNS OF BEHAVIOR

For being predefined, habitual action has a typical meaning which becomes a part of the general stock of knowledge taken for granted in a given society (Berger and Luckmann 1966, 53). When those typifications are reciprocal and performed by typical actors, institutionalization occurs since "any typification is an institution" (Berger and Luckmann 1966, 54).[5]

Social institutions are objective schemes of references (Schutz 1964, 7) consisting in a kind of knowledge at hand "determined by the systems of motivational relevances prevailing at the time in any situation" that makes it possible for us to achieve our purposes, obtaining the intended results through preestablished procedures (Schutz 2011, 177). This knowledge, in turn, is symbolic in nature:

> institutionalized social relations are [. . .] not real entities within the province of meaning of the everyday life-world but constructs of commonsense thinking that belong to a different subuniverse, perhaps that which W. James called the subuniverse of ideal relations. For this reason, we can apprehend them only symbolically; but the symbols appresenting these entities themselves pertain to the paramount reality of the life-world and motivate our actions within it. (Schutz and Luckmann 1989, 291)

As human beings, we are born into a world of social institutions in which "we have to find our bearings" and with which "we have to come to terms" (Schutz and Luckmann 1989, 237). Thus, institutions are a part of the social world naively accepted in the natural attitude, a world that was created by the alter egos, to whose existence we orient our activities (Schutz 1964, 5);

and—as seen in chapter 2—"any in-group has a relatively natural concept of the world which its members take for granted" (Schutz 1964, 121).

More precisely, three main features can be distinguished in Schutz's account. Social institutions refer to other people's mental activity, they allow us to master our daily life, and they are composed of typified patterns of social interactions that are distinctive of group life. Let us consider each of these traits in some detail.

First, institutions are social things designed for a purpose by other human beings (Schutz 1964,10). Thus, "in their meaning and origin," they "refer to human actions [. . .] to its meaning for the person who orients his behavior by it" (Schutz and Luckmann 1989, 208). Insofar as they were "created by other people's activity," they have their own "history, genesis, and construction" (Schutz 1964, 71). For instance, social institutions "refer to the world of my contemporaries [. . .] or point back to the world of my predecessors [. . .] because I can always interpret them as testimony to the conscious life of human beings [. . .] who adhered to these institutions" (Schutz 1964, 43).

Second, institutions are a part of the organized patterns of routines that allow us to master most of the problems of daily life without the "need to define or redefine situations which have occurred so many times or to look for new solutions of old problems hitherto handled satisfactorily" (Schutz 1964, 108). As Thomason (1982, 102) notes, Schutz refers to "the different degrees of institutionalization" obtained in various societies and in particular sectors of the same society: the firmness of institutions varies according to "the degree to which reciprocal schemes of typifications are employed." For Schutz, "the more instituzionalized or standardized a behavior pattern is, [. . .] the greater is the chance that my own self-typifying behavior will bring about the state of affairs aimed at" (Schutz 1962, 26).

Third, institutions are a kind of "cultural pattern of group life" (Schutz 1964, 92) which the individual has to interiorize and use in order to "define his personal unique situation" and fulfill his particular, personal interests (Schutz 1964, 253). These patterns mainly consist of typifications and relevances that define objective meanings; for instance, social roles and role expectations (Schutz 1964, 253).

So, institutions are for Schutz a kind of knowledge at hand determined by the system of motivational relevances prevailing in any situation which makes it possible for a person to achieve his purposes at hand, obtaining the intended results through preestablished procedures. They are also a part of the social world naively accepted in the natural attitude of the in-group; that is, they belong to the relative natural concept of the world taken for granted by its members. More specifically, institutions are composed of typified patterns of social interactions which are distinctive of group life. They are an organized pattern of routines that allow people to master the problems of daily life without the need of redefining situations that have occurred many times before or of looking for new solutions to old problems that have already been handled satisfactorily. And institutions are cultural patterns of group life consisting of typifications and relevances that define objective meanings such as social roles and role expectations, among others.

When institutions are crystallized, they are "experienced as existing over and beyond the individuals who 'happen to' embody them at the moment," as if they possessed "a reality of their own" that "confronts the individual as an external and coercive fact" (Berger and Luckmann 1966, 58). Even if institutions are the product of human activity, once established they present themselves as endowed with objectivity.

Consequently, on one side, *in status nascendi*, "institutions are constructed and maintained" in interactions endowed with a "tenuous" objectivity which means that they can be "easily changeable" (Berger and Luckmann 1966, 58). In other words, they remain "fairly accessible to deliberate intervention" by those who have constructed them and thus retain "the possibility of changing them or even abolishing them" for being alone responsible for having constructed and shaped this world "in the course of a shared biography which they can remember" (Berger and Luckmann 1966, 58–59). On the other side, "all this changes in the process of transmission to the new generation," which "had no part in shaping it" (Berger and Luckmann 1966, 59). "A world so regarded attains a firmness in consciousness; it becomes real in an ever more massive way and it can no longer be changed so readily" (Berger and Luckmann 1966, 59). For those who did not construct this world but inherit it, "it becomes *the* world"; in comparison to those who created it, for whom it "loses its playful quality and becomes 'serious'" (Berger and Luckmann 1966, 59; Berger and Luckmann's emphasis). That is why the world constructed by the parents becomes partially opaque "like nature" for their children since they took no part in shaping it (Berger and Luckmann 1966, 59).

So, institutions appear as "given, unalterable and self-evident" (Berger and Luckmann 1966, 59). "An institutional world, then, is experienced as an objective reality" whose history "antedates the individual's birth and is not accessible to his biographical recollection" (Berger and Luckmann 1966, 60). Institutions are "historical and objective facticities" that confront us "as an episode located within the objective history of society": they are out there as external, persistent realities that resist any attempt "to change or evade them" (Berger and Luckmann 1966, 60). We cannot "wish them away" because they exert a coercive power over us (Berger and Luckmann 1966, 60). It flows that:

> Since institutions exist as external reality, the individual cannot understand them by introspection. He must "go out" and learn about them, just as he must to learn

about nature. This remains true even though the social world, as a humanly produced reality, is potentially understandable in a way not possible in the case of
the natural world. (Berger and Luckmann 1966, 60)

How come, being humanly produced realities, institutions end up being
incomprehensible? According to Berger and Luckmann, this is so because
institutions are objectivated products of human activity.

The institutional world is objectivated human activity, and so is every single
institution. In other words, despite the objectivity that marks the social world in
human experience, it does not thereby acquire an ontological status apart from
the human activity that produced it. (Berger and Luckmann 1966, 60–61)

The process of objectivation of human activity is, in turn, produced by a
consciousness that retains part of our experience "as recognizable and memorable entities," which is then sedimented (Berger and Luckmann 1966, 67). In
addition to this kind of sedimentation, operated by an individual consciousness, intersubjective sedimentation occurs "when several individuals share a
common biography, experiences of which become incorporated in a common
stock of knowledge" (Berger and Luckmann 1966, 67). Also, intersubjective
sedimentation turns into social sedimentation when it is objectivated in a sign
system because then "the possibility of reiterated objectification of the shared
experiences arises" (Berger and Luckmann 1966, 67), which makes it "likely
that these experiences will be transmitted from one generation to the next, and
from one collectivity to another" (Berger and Luckmann 1966, 68).

With objectivation in "an objectively available sign system," a transformation occurs in the sedimented experience. It acquires "a status of incipient
anonymity" by being detached "from their original context of concrete individual biographies" and become "generally available to all who share, or may
share in the future, in the sign system in question" (Berger and Luckmann
1966, 68). This way, experiences become easier to transmit. Even if any sign
system would do, usually the linguistic system is the decisive.

Language objectivates the shared experiences and makes them available to all
within the linguistic community, thus becoming both the basis and the instru-
ment of the collective stock of knowledge. Furthermore, language provides the
means for objectifying new experiences, allowing their incorporation into the
already existing stock of knowledge, and it is the most important means by
which the objectivated and objectified sedimentations are transmitted in the
tradition of the collectivity in question. (Berger and Luckmann 1966, 68)

As a consequence of its sedimentation, its designation and transmission in
a linguistic system, experience becomes accessible for those who never had it,

since linguistic designation "abstracts the experience from its individual bio-graphical occurrences" and turns into "an objective possibility for everyone" (Berger and Luckmann 1966, 68). This means that it becomes anonymous and integrates the common stock of knowledge. Thus, through objectiva-tion, experience "becomes an objective possibility for everyone" (Berger and Luckmann 1966, 68) that can be incorporated to a larger tradition, it can also be taught to new generations and even be diffused in collectivities totally different from the one in which this experience was generated and originally transmitted. "Language becomes the depository of a large aggregate of col-lective sedimentations, which can be acquired monothetically, that is, as cohesive wholes and without reconstructing their original process of forma-tion" since "the actual origin of the sedimentations" becomes "unimportant" (Berger and Luckmann 1966, 69).

Summarizing, human action tends to become habitual through repetition. This means that it becomes typical and comprehensible for others. Once habitualities get crystallized, social institutions emerge and they are more stable and permanent than actions per se. Thus, institutions tend to be experi-enced as objective realities that exert coercion and control on the individuals, being practically unalterable. When this process of objectification is retained in consciousness, it tends to settle as stereotyped, and its meaning is sedi-mented. In the cases in which this meaning is shared, it is intersubjectively sedimented; in the cases in which it is objectivated in a sign system, it is socially sedimented. Generally speaking, language is the sign system used for that, since it makes the sedimented experience accessible to others and avail-able for future generations in the mode of anonymous types that transform it qualitatively by depriving it of its individual biographical context and by making it accessible to all.

For being "a reciprocal typification of habitualized actions by types of actors," institutions serve to "control human conduct by setting up predefined patterns of conduct, which channel it in one direction as against the many other directions that would theoretically be possible" (Thomason 1982, 110, 105). Institutions "alone can pattern and channel human conduct in such a way as to preclude successfully that overwhelming 'problem of choice' which man's openness to the world would pose if left unchecked" (Thomason 1982, 104).

The aforesaid implies that "institutions work as controls for human behav-ior" (Thomason 1982, 102), that is, "they 'close' the world-openness of man, just to the extent that they take on an objective, independent, thing-like exis-tence" (Thomason 1982, 105). Hence, institutions are reifications that "pro-vide ready-made channels or grooves for human conduct, i.e., unquestioned patterns which resolve quasi-automatically the 'problems of choice' that man would otherwise face" (Thomason 1982, 106). Yet, one can go further and say along with Berger and Pullberg (1965, 201) that the "ultimate root" of the processes of reification of institutions lies in "some fundamental terrors of human existence, notably the terror of chaos—which is then assuaged by the fabrication of the sort of firm order that only reifications can constitute."

Institutions, then, are key for mastering everyday life. Once we attribute to them "a kind of taken-for-granted facticity, our social world becomes a structure of 'dominations.' We are constrained and channeled by our own constructions" (Thomason 1982, 107). Constructions, in turn, make it possible for us to establish routines.

> People live according to certain routines. These are built upon standardized typifications which are broadly accepted within the social collectivity. Such routines and typifications constitute effective institutional channels just in so far as they are left unquestioned and granted a certain thing-like autonomy. Without institutional channels, and without taken-for-granted reifications, the social world would be devoid of sustantive content. (Thomason 1982, 107)

It follows that, in order for institutions to accomplish their specific goals, they have to be reified, that is, they must refer "to a certain attributed thing-like objectivity" (Thomason 1982, 131). Generally speaking, reification is

> a cognitive process whereby various aspects of experience come to acquire a kind of inappropriate ontological fixedness. Reification, in other words, involves "thing-ification" (*Verdinglichung*): the attribution of "facticity," concreteness, authonomy, impersonality, objectivity, externality etc., to the "things" that are reified. These attributions must be inappropriate. The things reified must *not* be the concrete, autonomous, inert facticities they are taken to be. (Thomason 1982, 88)

People reify experienced objectivities whenever they ignore that the latter are constituted and therefore "dependent upon various subjective processes" (Thomason 1982, 90). When this occurs, "people take the objectivity of their experience for granted" (Thomason 1982, 90).

In this sense, reification also implies a process of mystification: "Institutions are reified by mystifying their true character as human objectivations and by defining them, again, as supra-human facticities analogous to the facticities of nature" (Berger and Pullberg 1965, 207). Accordingly, "the deviant from these institutionally defined courses of action may thus be perceived [. . .] as one who offends against the very nature of 'things,' against the 'natural order' of the world or of his own being" (Berger and Pullberg 1965, 207).

Summing up, institutions are typified, unquestioned patterns of action which consist in organized, regularized, and stabilized social relationships. They, as it were, quasi-automatically resolve "the problem of choice" for people and make it possible for them to accomplish their specific goals and master their everyday life. Institutions are thus reifications that provide ready-made channels for human conduct. Reification, in turn, involves the attribution of facticity, concreteness, autonomy, impersonality, objectivity, externality and the like to a product of human action. Reified institutions are seen as "things"—which they are not. Thus, reifications are inappropriate attributions or, as we may say, mystifications. The reified things are not concrete, autonomous, inert factiticities; they are not the things they are taken to be. To reify something, then, means to ignore that experienced objectivities, such as institutions, are constituted by subjective processes. Reification is an *improper* objectification that does not respect the nature of things. It is not that the subjective actually becomes objective. Rather, it is just that human activity can be improperly grasped as if it were a thing. Put otherwise, social institutions involve always a mystification of human activity.

FROM THE *EGO AGENS* TO SOCIAL INSTITUTIONS: A SYNTHESIS OF SOME MAJOR FINDINGS IN PHENOMENOLOGICAL SOCIOLOGY

We have seen that Schutz conceives of *pragma* as the *pragma* of the *ego agens*. *Pragmata* are always the *pragmata* of a self at work. Social personalities are a product of the *ego* working on its *pragma*. Moreover, social personalities are not persons constituted in full but partial personalities which rely on the *ego agens*. Consequently, they do not act on their own. It is the *ego agens* which acts through them. Indeed, *pragmata* belong to the *ego agens* who constitutes the social personalities, which in turn only act in a secondary, metaphorical way and by no means can act back on its *pragmata*. This indicates that the substratum of *pragmata* is the *ego agens*, which is also its *origo* and, through them, the *origo* of all my dead selves and of all my social personalities.

However, it does not mean that the ego constitutes social personalities freely and in absolute loneliness. They are the *result* of our participation in social circles constituted by parts of personalities of the individuals integrating them, whose total personalities remain outside the common area of social circles. In accordance, *pragmata* are twofold realities: they have a subjective, immanent dimension but also an objective, transcendent one. The former has an identity and systemic properties, the latter is schizophrenic-like and multiple; one of them acts, the other is just a mask for acting.

The key concept here is "reiterability." *Pragmata* are reiterable not only by the same *ego agens* that originated them but also by other *egos*. That is why Schutz speaks of the transferability of *pragmata* as a condition of the development of a social *habitus*. Habitualities, then, play an important role in the constitution and stabilization of the system of our social attitudes. The more habitualized the different levels of the social persons are, the more we share experiencings of our own *pragmata* and of their transferability. This is what allows us to have a habitus—which, by the way, is a set of generalized schemes of comportment that can be transferred from one *ego agens* to another. It is the reiterability of analogous *pragma*, facilitated by the stabilization of shared social attitudes, what constitutes the social personalities, which are an interplay of subjective and objective aspects, real and irreal, actual and potential. This is the reason why the *ego agens* is split up and teared apart: because it has to mediate between *durée* and social time, inner and outer experiences, the individual and the social; briefly, the subjective and the objective.

The partitioning of the *ego* into multiple social personalities—what Schutz calls "the hypothesis of the schizophrenic ego"—is the starting point for a conceptualization of social roles. In this view, it is the *ego agens* who decides which of its several selves will operate in a certain area of the social world and therefore which role will it assume.

Each social personality corresponds to a specific area of the social world experienced by who assumes a given role from a central position. Relatedly, social personalities are peripheral manifestations of the core of the self (or heart of a person). Therefore, split experiences of the actor's partial personalities are counteracted by the individual's consciousness, and the individual sees himself in all his sequential and substantially differentiated participations, and experiences himself as the center of the social world.

Because of their relationship with the self, social roles involve a self-typification on the part of the incumbent. It is him who, up to a certain point, typifies his own situation in the social world and the relations he has with his peers and with cultural objects.

The ability to self-typify originates in a particularity of the spiritual subject consisting of the emergence of the apperception of the self whereby the ego is at the same time a subject and an "object": on one hand, he is the ego conscious of being a self; on the other hand, he is the person constituted by and for this self.

By virtue of this ability, the individual can choose the attitude to adopt toward the role that he assumes within the group. From this perspective, roles are attitudes that we assume voluntarily in everyday life as resources that we can use. According to how the individual defines his situation, the different roles of his multiple memberships of social groups will be experienced as a set of self-typifications arranged in a private order of domains of changing relevance. However, the roles and role expectations that the *ego agens* considers elements of his network of typifications are formed mostly by others and are accepted as such by the group to which he belongs. Thus, the individual defines his role through a system of typifications and relevances that he shares with others.

The acceptance of a system of common relevances leads the members of a group to homogenous self-typification. Such individuals who find their positioning in the group must also be aware of the typical behaviors, actions, and motives that can be expected from others according to the roles that they play. At the same time, learning the social roles and behavioral expectations typical of those who assume them is necessary for assuming proper roles and for exhibiting due behavior to obtain approval because other members of the in-group expect that he or she who assumes a role acts in the typical manner defined for that given role. It is worth saying that a social role comes with a set of expectations that the person assuming it must fulfill.

Role expectations consist of typifications of interaction patterns that serve as socially approved ways of solving typical problems that are often institutionalized and therefore ordered in domains of relevance with a particular order originating in the relative natural conception of the world held by the group. Roles are a part of the relative natural conception of the world of groups. They take part in the formation of social types and integrate socioculturally derived knowledge. Also, they belong to socially derived domains of relevances and can even contribute to generating processes of institutionalization.

Social institutions are a kind of knowledge at hand determined by the prevalent systems of motivational relevances. More specifically, they are a kind of cultural pattern of group life to be interiorized by individuals and to be used by them in order to define their situation in the group and fulfill their personal interests. These patterns mainly consist of typifications and relevances that define objective meanings. Thus, they are not real entities but ideal relations which consist in constructs of commonsense thinking that can only be apprehended by symbols. Symbols, however, represent real entities pertaining to the life-world that actually motivate our actions in it. They are a part of the social world naively accepted in the natural attitude.

As typified patterns of meaning, social institutions produce a "closing" of the human world that channels human conduct and makes it possible for us to achieve our purposes at hand, obtaining the intended results through preestablished procedures. The more institutionalized or standardized a behavior pattern is, the greater is the chance that a self-typifying behavior will bring about the state of affairs aimed at. Accordingly, social institutions are a part of the organized patterns of routines that allow us to master the problems of daily life without the need to define or redefine ordinary situations or to look for solutions anew each time we act.

Social institutions are intersubjectively produced. Nevertheless, once they exist, they tend to "harden" and solidify, thereby acquiring the appearance of objectivities, which are deemed to have coercive power over human beings. Seen this way, social institutions are characterized by their exteriority and moral coercion. The individual experiences them as objective realities possessing a reality of their own, as if they were rock-solid, external and unalterable things.

Consequently, social institutions are reifications. Reification is a cognitive process whereby experience comes to acquire an inappropriate ontological fixedness. The things reified must not be the kind of things they are taken to be. To reify something means to ignore that experienced objectivities are constituted and therefore dependent upon subjective processes. This, in turn, involves a mystification since it implies conceiving institutions as supra-human facticities, not as human objectivations. Reification, then, is an inappropriate attribution of a thing-like nature to a product of human activity. They are typified patterns of human behavior perceived as natural things.

In conclusion, we may say that phenomenological sociology is not limited to a micro description of face-to-face relationships. It can perfectly account for the realm of the social in its full extent. As a matter of fact, we have started this chapter from the most intimate experience involved in sociality—namely, the *ego agens* working on its *pragma*—and went all the way through to the most impersonal, dehumanized form—which is institutions that have been reified and mystified to the limit of forgetting the subjective origins of those forms of behavior now perceived as objective and external to whom, nonetheless, created them. This transition is possible because of the dual character of *pragma,* which is already involved in the acting of the *ego* and its pragmatic unification and yet persists in social institutions, no matter how objectified they are. For being subjective as well as objective, *pragmata* allow the phenomenological sociologist to cover the whole range of his peculiar realm of research. For this reason, we may well conclude this chapter claiming that phenomenological sociology has a distinctive pragmatic air.

NOTES

1. I offer an extensive, systematic account of Schutz's concepts of *ego agens* and *pragma* in my paper "On the Reiterability of Pragmata" (Belvedere 2015b).

2. Schutz's notion of habitus, as well as Husserl's (which will be addressed next), not only are worthy in themselves. They have interesting consequences for the debate in contemporary sociology, specially regarding the work of Pierre Bourdieu. I explore those consequences in "The habitus made me do it" (Belvedere 2013c).

3. Even though Schutz does not mention it, his description of how the reiterableness of analogous *pragma* works is quite similar to Husserl's argument that intersubjectivity is based on the past experiences of my own transcendental *ego* (see San Martín 2008, 8–9). Schutz's argument is that "the sedimented experience is a *pragma* (e.g., kinaesthesias) accomplished by *me*, in the memory of which this potentiality (reality in the mode of probability) proves to be an earlier core of reality: once this *hinc*, now a 'phenomenon of probability,' was a reality for me, but a reality *illinc*. For by my pragma my earlier *hinc* has now become an *illinc*" (Schutz 2013, 226).

4. Schutz's concept of social roles may well be addressed as a subject in its own right. I do that in a recent paper (Belvedere 2019). Here, instead, I will briefly consider it in relation to a wider range of problems.

5. The phenomenology of social institutions is one of the most important contributions of the Schutzian perspective to the social sciences. There is more to it than what can be exposed in this chapter. An extended presentation of this perspective in contemporary context can be found in Belvedere and Gros (2019).

Epilogue

A Manifesto for Phenomenological Sociology

The aim of this book has been to demonstrate the very existence of phenomenological sociology. Its starting point has been the current debate about the possibility of such a science. It has been proved that not only adversaries, but also respected phenomenologists, agree that phenomenology is not a science but a philosophy and that, at most, it can be a proto-scientific endeavor. Fortunately, some others agree that it is a distinctive kind of social science furnished with a repertory of concepts and methods different from those of "good old school" sociology. Seen this way, phenomenological sociology is not just another way of doing sociology but an alternate to mainstream sociology.

In order to describe this paradigm, questions concerning its object and method have been addressed. It has been argued that the specific object of phenomenological sociology is the natural attitude of groups, which is constituted through a structuration of the field of consciousness through imposed relevances of the in-group upon its members and upon out-groups. To deal with such attitude, phenomenological sociology begins with the description of the *epoché* of the natural attitude of groups. However, the natural attitude can also be altered, whether spontaneously—for instance, as a result of social conflicts; whether experimentally—as in breaching experiments such as those conducted by ethnomethodologists. Once described the natural attitude, eidetic analysis can be performed, which consists in describing its constancies, that is, its intrinsic configuration and structure. It follows constitutive analysis, whose aim is to disclose the congregational work of producing a local order endowed with endogenous properties which are the outcome of member's cooperation.

As it has been illustrated in this book, steps of this method have been practiced in sociology for about two hundred years now. Therefore, the method of phenomenological sociology is an established practice. However, this practice has been fragmentary and lacked reflection. Examples have been

provided of how numerous phenomenologists and sociologists have performed one or another step. Yet it is hard to find instantiations of the use of
the complete method delineated here, except for the author's research experience. Consequently, the program of phenomenological sociology had not
been outlined in full until the publication of this book, whose main contribution has been to systematize and *mettre en valeur* this perspective.

This does not mean to create *ex nihilo* a new science or anything alike. On
the contrary, it involves the acknowledgment and praise of a tacit knowledge,
bringing to light a wealth of good practices in sociological inquiry that have
been overlooked and neglected for two centuries. Outlining the program of
phenomenological sociology is not to propose a "new sociological method"
but to assume an ongoing tradition of tacit practices and procedures which—
as things themselves do—first started by existing on its own, pre-reflectively,
and only after that come to be thought and systematized.

Not only its practice and method have been displayed here but also a
consolidated tradition of sedimented meanings and findings. Regardless its
fragmentary and occasioned character, the practice of phenomenological
sociology has provided a coherent, consistent, and productive body of knowledge based on more than a century of accounts and descriptions of lived experiences. The legacy of this tradition is a conception of social life grounded on
the *ego agens* as split-up into *durée* and cosmic time—that is, into subjective
and public time. Taking as a point of departure this teared apart subjectivity,
a gradient of relations going from familiarity to anonymity was described.
Along it, the different strata of social life were arranged, from habitualities
and face-to-face relationships up to institutions, social classes, and the state.

The productivity of this tradition well deserves to be praised. The best
way to do that is to propose a manifesto for phenomenological sociology.
Ten points will suffice to outline its program and proclaim its coming-to-age:

1. Phenomenological sociology is a science dealing with the natural attitude of groups.
2. It starts by describing what is taken for granted in a given group—i.e.,
   by describing what is considered relevant.
3. To describe the natural attitude of a group is to describe the system of
   imposed relevances that its members must take into account and that the
   group intends to impose upon other groups.
4. To describe the natural attitude of a group is not only to describe what
   is taken for granted in it but also what its members may call into question—this is, to describe how the natural attitude can be challenged.
5. The fact that the natural attitude can be challenged allows for an
   experimentation with it. Not only can it be naturally challenged in

everyday-life situations and social conflict, but also in experimental situations ideated by the phenomenological sociologist.

6. Both, natural and experimental challenges might lead or contribute to social change.

7. One among other manners in which phenomenological sociology has contributed to social change is by questioning and setting aside prejudices such as racism, sexism, social discrimination, and the like. To question what we take for granted in the natural attitude may help fight these and other prejudices.

8. The outcome of this challenge is not just a better view of society but *ipso facto* a new kind of group relationships. That is, phenomenological sociology, when conducted properly, does not provide just a better view on society but a better society, in the first place.

9. In accordance, phenomenological sociology is helpful for building up a democratic, integrated society where social justice might be achieved, and marginalized groups can get the dignity and recognition they claim.

10. For the above mentioned, phenomenological sociology is not just a theoretical perspective, neither a merely scientific approach, but also—and most significantly—a means for social change and human emancipation.

It is the author's best wish that this manifesto contributes to bring out the paradigm of phenomenological sociology as an ongoing centenary practice, that it inspires new generations to continue and delve into its wealth of treasures, and that it encourages its practitioners to involve in social change so that we can make a fair, equal world for all.

Bibliography

Arvidson, P. S. 2018. "The Field of Consciousness and Extended Cognition." *Human Studies* 41: 21–40.

Barber, Michael. 2012. "Why Ethnomethodology Needs the Transcendental Ego." In *Interaction and Everyday Life: Phenomenological and Ethnomethodological Essays in Honor of George Psathas*, edited by Hisashi Nasu and Frances Chaput Waksler, 153–167. Lanham, MD: Lexington.

———. 2017. *Religion and Humor as Emancipating Provinces of Meaning*. Cham, Switzerland: Springer.

———. 2021. "African-American Humor and Trust." *Human Studies* 44: 151–169.

Belvedere, Carlos. 2013a. "What Is Schutzian Phenomenology?" *Schutzian Research* 5: 65–80.

———. 2013b. "On George Psathas and Phenomenological Sociology." *Schutzian Research* 5: 131–136.

———. 2013c. "The Habitus Made Me Do It: Bourdieu's Key Concept as a Substruction of the Monad." *Philosophy Study* 3, 12: 1094–1108.

———. 2015a. "Durkheim as the Founding Father of Phenomenological Sociology." *Human Studies* 38: 369–390.

———. 2015b. "On the Reiterability of Pragmata: A Schutzian 'Alternate' to the Sociological Concept of 'Practice.'" *Società, Mutamento, Politica. Rivista Italiana di Sociologia* 6, 12: 97–115.

———. 2016. "Why I Cannot Dance the Tango: Reflections of an Incompetent Member of the 'milongas porteñas.'" *Schutzian Research* 8: 179–200.

———. 2017. "Lester Embre on 'Collective Subjects.'" *Schutizan Research* 9, 2017: 79–84.

———. 2019. "Alfred Schutz's Fragments on Social Roles as a Phenomenological Alternate to Mainstream Sociology." *Human Studies* 42, 3: 327–342.

———. 2020. "Ethnomethodology as an Experimentation with the Natural Attitude: George Psathas on Phenomenological Sociology." *Human Studies* 43, 3: 353–360.

————. 2021. "Topic Relevance as the Basic Structuration of the Field of Consciousness." *Sociologia e Ricerca Sociale* 124: 37–51.

Belvedere, Carlos and Alexis Gros. 2019. "The Phenomenology of Social Institutions in the Schutzian Tradition." *Schutzian Research* 11: 43–74.

Berger, Peter L. 2011. *The Sacred Canopy. Elements of a Sociological Theory of Religion.* New York: Open Road.

Berger, Peter and Stanley Pullberg. 1965. "Reification and the Sociological Critique of Consciousness." *History and Theory* 4 (2): 196–211.

Berger, Peter L. and Thomas Luckmann. 1966. *The Social Construction of Reality: A Treatise in the Sociology of Knowledge.* New York: Anchor.

Buttler, Judith. 1990. "Performative Acts and Gender Constitution: An Essay in Phenomenology and Feminist Theory." In *Performing Feminisms. Feminist Critical Theory and Theatre*, edited by Sue-Ellen Case, 270–282. Baltimore and London: The Johns Hopkins University Press.

Cortázar, Julio. 2019. *Rayuela.* Madrid: Real Academia Española y Asociación de Academias de la Lengua Española.

Cox, Ronald R. 1978. *Schutz's Theory of Relevance: A Phenomenological Critique.* The Hague / Boston / London: Martinus Nijhoff.

Dreher, Jochen. 2012. "Chapter 10. Investigating Friendship: A Prospective Dispute between Protosociology and Phenomenological Sociology." In *Interaction and Everyday Life: Phenomenological and Ethnomethodological Essays in Honor of George Psathas*, edited by Hisashi Nasu and Frances Chaput Waksler, 153–167. Lanham, MD: Lexington.

Durkheim, Emile. 1999. *Les règales de la méthode sociologique* [The Rules of Sociological Method]. Paris: Quadrige / Presses Universitaires de France.

————. 2004a. *De la division du travail social* [The Division of Labour in Society]. Paris: Quadrige / Presses Universitaires de France.

————. 2004b. *Sociologie et philosophie* [Sociology and Philosophy]. Paris: Quadrige / Presses Universitaires de France.

————. 2005. *Le suicide* [Suicide]. Paris: Quadrige / Presses Universitaires de France.

Eberle, Thomas. 2012. "Chapter 9. Phenomenology and Sociology. Divergent Interpretations of a Complex Relationship." In *Interaction and Everyday Life: Phenomenological and Ethnomethodological Essays in Honor of George Psathas*, edited by Hisashi Nasu and Frances Chaput Waksler, 135–152. Lanham, MD: Lexington.

Embree, Lester. 2008. "The Nature and Role of Phenomenological Psychology in Alfred Schutz." *Journal of Phenomenological Pshychology*, 39: 141–150.

————. 2009a. "Dorion Cairns and Alfred Schutz on the Egological Reduction." In *Alfred Schutz and His Intellectual Partners*, edited by Hisashi Nasu, Lester Embree, George Psathas, and Ilja Srubar, 177–216. Konstanz: UVK Verlagsgesellschaft mbH.

————. 2009b. "Some Philosophical Differences within a Friendship: Gurwitsch and Schutz." In *Alfred Schutz and His Intellectual Partners,* edited by Hisashi

Nasu, Lester Embree, George Psathas, Ilja Srubar, 231–253. Konstanz: UVK Verlagsgesellschaft mbH.

———. 2010. "From 'We' to 'I' and Back: Still Learning from the New School." In *The 41ST Annual Meeting of The Husserl Circle*. New York City: The New School for Social Research, 37–46.

———. 2011. "Groups in Schutz: The Concrete Meaning Structure of the Socio-Historical World." *Journal of Existential and Phenomenological Theory and Culture* 6, 1: 1–11.

———. 2015. *The Schutzian Theory of the Cultural Sciences*. Cham, Heidelberg, New York: Dordrecht and London: Springer.

———, ed. 1988. *Worldly Phenomenology: The Continuing Influence of Alfred Schutz on North American Human Science*. Washington: CARP and University Press of America.

Garfinkel, Harold. 1994. *Studies in Ethnomethodology.* Oxford: Polity Press.

———. 2002. *Ethnomethodology's Program: Working Out Durkheim's Aphorism.* Lanham, MD: Rowman & Littlefield.

Garfinkel, Harold and Harvey Sacks. 1986. "On Formal Structures of Practical Actions." In *Ethnomethodological Studies of Work*, edited by Harold Garfinkel, 157–189. London: Routledge.

Giorgi, Amadeo. 2020. "In Defense of Scientific Phenomenologies." *Journal of Phenomenological Psychology* 51 (2020): 135–161.

Gordon, Lewis R. 1995. *Fanon and the Crisis of European Man. An Essay on Philosophy and the Human Sciences.* New York and London: Routledge.

———. 2000. *Existentia Africana: Understanding Africana Existential Thought.* New York and London: Routledge.

———. 2008. *An Introduction to Africana Philosophy.* New York: Cambridge University Press.

Göttlich, Andreas. 2014. "Relevancias impuestas y relevancias libres. Una mirada sociológica acerca de la teoría de la relevancia de Alfred Schutz." In *Fenomenología del poder*, edited by Jochen Dreher and Daniela Griselda López, 87–109. Bogotá: Universidad Santo Tomás.

Heidegger, Martin. 1998. *Pathmarks.* New York: Cambridge University Press.

Heritage, John. 1992. *Garfinkel and Ethnomethodology.* Cambridge: Polity Press.

Hindess, Barry. 2006. "The 'Phenomenological' Sociology of Alfred Schutz." *Economy and Society* 1 (1): 1–27.

Husserl, Edmund. 1970. *The Crisis of European Sciences and Transcendental Phenomenology.* Evanston, IL: Northwestern University Press.

———. 1982. *Cartesian Meditations: An Introduction to Phenomenology.* The Hage: Martinus Nijhoff.

———. 1991. *On the Phenomenology of the Consciousness of Internal Time.* Dordrecht: Kluwer Academic Publishers.

———. 2005. *Ideas relativas a una fenomenología pura y una filosofía fenomenológica. Libro segundo: Investigaciones fenomenológicas sobre la constitución.* [Ideas II]. México: Fondo de Cultura Económica.

———. 2006. *Meditaciones Cartesianas* [Cartesian Meditations]. Madrid: Tecnos.

Kersten, Fred. 2010. Introduction. *Schutzian Research* 2: 61–62.

López Sáenz, María del Carmen. 1995. "La sociofenomenología de A. Schütz: entre el constructivismo y el realismo," *Papers*, 47: 55–74.

Lynch, Michael. 1999. "Silence in Context: Ethnomethodology and Social Theory." *Human Studies* 22: 211–233.

Martínez, María Teresa. 2007. *Pierre Bourdieu. Razones y Lecciones de una Práctica Sociológica. Del Estructuralismo Genético a la Sociología Reflexiva.* Buenos Aires: Manantial.

Mitchell, J. 2000. "Living a Lie: Self-deception, Habit, and Social Roles." *Human Studies* 23, 2: 145–156.

Morley, James. 2010. "It's Always About the *Epoché.*" In *The Redirection of Psychology: Essays in Honor of Amadeo P. Giorgi,* edited by T. F. Cloonan and C. Thiboutot, 223–232. Montreal: Cercle Interdisciplinaire de Recherches Phénoménologiques (CIRP).

Muzzetto, Luigi. 2006. *Il soggetto e il sociale. Alfred Schutz e il mondo "taken for granted."* Milan: Franco Angeli.

Overgaard, Soren and Dan Zahavi. 2009. "Phenomenological Sociology—The Subjectivity of Everyday Life." In *Encountering the Everyday: An Introduction to the Sociologies of the Unnoticed,* edited by Michael Hviid Jacobsen, 93–115. Basingstoke: Palgrave Macmillan.

Paoletti, Giovanni. 2002. "Durkheim et le problème de l'objetivité: une lecture des *Formes élémentaires de la vie religieuse.*" *Revue Française de Sociologie* 43 (3): 437–459.

Psathas, George. 1968. "Ethnomethods and Phenomenology." *Social Research* 35 (3): 500–520.

———. 1973. Introduction. In *Phenomenological Sociology: Issues and Applications,* edited by George Psathas, 1–21. New York: Wiley.

———. 2004. "Alfred Schutz's Influence on American Sociologists and Sociology." *Human Studies* 27: 1–35.

———. 2009. "The Correspondence of Alfred Schutz and Harold Garfinkel: What Was the 'Terra Incognita' and the 'Treasure Island'?" In *Alfred Schutz and His Intellectual Partners,* edited by Hisashi Nasu, Lester Embree, George Psathas, and Ilja Srubar, 401–433. Konstanz: UVK Vergesellschaft, mbH.

———. 2012. "On Garfinkel and Schutz: Contacts and Influence." *Schutzian Research* 4: 23–31.

Sacks, Harvey. 1995. *Lecctures on Conversation,* Volumes 1 and 2. Malden, Oxford, Victoria: Blackwell.

San Martín, Javier. 2008. *La fenomenología de Husserl como utopía de la razón. Introducción a la fenomenología.* Madrid: Biblioteca Nueva.

Schutz, Alfred. 1962. *Collected Papers I. The Problem of Social Reality.* The Hague: Martinus Nijhoff.

———. 1964. *Collected Papers II. Studies in Social Theory.* The Hague: Martinus Nijhoff.

———. 1966. *Collected Papers III: Studies in Phenomenological Philosophy.* The Hage: Martinus Nijhoff.

———. 1967. *The Phenomenology of the Social World.* Evanston, IL: Northwestern University Press.

———. 1996. *Collected Papers IV.* Dordrecht: Kluwer.

———. 2010. "Problems of a Sociology of Language (Fall semester, 1958)." *Schutzian Research* 2: 55–107.

———. 2011. *Collected Papers V. Phenomenology and the Social Sciences.* Dordrecht, Heidelberg, New York, London: Springer.

———. 2013. *Collected Papers VI. Literary Reality and Relationships.* Dordrecht, Heidelberg, New York, London: Springer.

Schutz, Alfred, and Thomas Luckmann. 1989. *The Structures of the Life-World*, Volume 2. Evanston, IL: Northwestern University Press.

Spiegelberg, Herbert. 1980. "Putting Ourselves into the Place of Others: Toward a Phenomenology of Imaginary Self Transposal." *Human Studies* 3 (2): 169–173.

Stedman Jones, Sue. 2003. "Représentations." *Durkheimian Studies* 9: 14–19.

———. 2007. "Functionalism of Mind and Functionalism of Society: The Concept of Conscience and Durkheim's *Division of Social Labour*." *Durkheimian Studies* 13: 85–104.

Storm Heter, T. 2006. "Authenticity and Others: Sartre's Ethics of Recognition." *Sartre Studies International* 12 (2): 17–43.

Thomason, Burke C. 1982. *Making Sense of Reification. Alfred Schutz and Constructionist Theory.* New Jersey: Humanities Press.

Vaitkus, Steven. 2005. "The 'Naturality' of Alfred Schutz's Natural Attitude of the Life-World." In *Explorations of the Life-World: Continuing Dialogues with Alfred Schutz*, edited by Hisashi Nasu, Lester Embree, George Psathas, and Ilja Srubar, 97–121. Dordrecht: Springer.

Waksler, Frances Chaput. 1969. "Is a Phenomenological Sociology Possible?" Unpublished manuscript.

———. 2010. *The New Orleans Sniper. A Phenomenological Case Study of Constituting the Other.* Lanham, MD: University Press of America.

Warfield Rawls, Anne. 2002. Editor's Introduction. In *Ethnomethodology's Program: Working Out Durkheim's Aphorism*, Harold Garfinkel, 1–64. Lanham, MD: Rowman & Littlefield.

Yu, Chung-Chi. 2007. "On Schutz's Way of Doing Phenomenology: The Phenomenological Psychology of Husserl as a Clue." In *Phenomenology 2005: Selected Essays from Asia*, Volume 1, edited by Cheung Chan-Fai and Yu Chung-Chi, 757–766. Bucharest: Zeta Books.

———. 2014. "Mutual Tuning-In Relationships and Phenomenological Psychology." In *The Interrelation of Phenomenology, Social Sciences and the Arts*, edited by Michael Barber and Jochen Dreher, 229–242. Cham, Switzerland: Springer.

Index

About the Author

Carlos Belvedere received a PhD in Social Sciences. He holds a degree in Sociology as well as a degree in Philosophy. He is a tenured associate professor at the University of Buenos Aires and chair of the Philosophy Department at the National University of General Sarmiento. His areas of interest are phenomenological philosophy and sociological theory. He has authored several books and papers in the field of social phenomenology. He serves as associate editor in the journal *Schutzian Research*. He is a former co-chair of the Society for Phenomenology and the Human Sciences. He has recently published *El Coure*, a book on the phenomenology of tango.

9 781666 906127